Integrating Social and Emotional Learning with Content

This book provides a framework for creatively and effectively teaching social and emotional learning across content areas in grades 3–5 using illustrated texts such as graphic novels, manga, and picture books.

Thoughtful book choices that reflect the range of diversities found in classrooms and communities help support students as they develop their academic skills, and provide opportunities to address their unique socio-emotional needs. Covering theoretical context, the benefits of using graphic texts to activate important cognitive structures, as well as specific techniques and advice for implementation, this book makes pairing effective, diverse books with thoughtfully designed, standards-aligned lessons encouragingly simple.

Packed with adaptable lesson plans, book lists, differentiated activities and more, this book is a must read for educators seeking truly integrated learning experiences that meet all learners' academic and social and emotional learning (SEL) needs.

Sarah Bright, PhD, is a research associate at Northwestern University's Center for Talent Development and a post-doctoral research associate at Purdue University, where she works on research focusing on expanding the access of underrepresented gifted students to advanced programming and the impact of technology on learning. She is the co-author with Dr. Katherine Kapustka of *Integrating Social and Emotional Learning with Content: Using Picture Books for Differentiated Teaching in K-3 Classrooms* (Routledge, 2022).

Katherine Kapustka, Ed.D, is an associate professor of teacher education at DePaul University, where she also serves as the Director of Teacher Preparation, Leadership, and Licensure. She teaches a variety of courses in the elementary education program, including literacy and assessment. Her current research focuses on pre-service teachers' understanding of and attitudes toward differentiation in the classroom. She is the co-author with Dr. Sarah Bright of *Integrating Social and Emotional Learning with Content: Using Picture Books for Differentiated Teaching in K-3 Classrooms* (Routledge, 2022).

Integrating Social and Emotional Learning with Content

Using Graphic Texts for Differentiated Teaching in Grade 3–5 Classrooms

Sarah Bright, Ph.D. and Katherine Kapustka, Ed.D.

NEW YORK AND LONDON

First published 2025
by Routledge
605 Third Avenue, New York, NY 10158

and by Routledge
4 Park Square, Milton Park, Abingdon, Oxon, OX14 4RN

Routledge is an imprint of the Taylor & Francis Group, an informa business

© 2025 Sarah Bright and Katherine Kapustka

The right of Sarah Bright and Katherine Kapustka to be identified as authors of this work has been asserted in accordance with sections 77 and 78 of the Copyright, Designs and Patents Act 1988.

All rights reserved. No part of this book may be reprinted or reproduced or utilised in any form or by any electronic, mechanical, or other means, now known or hereafter invented, including photocopying and recording, or in any information storage or retrieval system, without permission in writing from the publishers.

Trademark notice: Product or corporate names may be trademarks or registered trademarks, and are used only for identification and explanation without intent to infringe.

Library of Congress Cataloging-in-Publication Data
Names: Bright, Sarah, author. | Kapustka, Katherine, author.
Title: Integrating social and emotional learning with content : using graphic texts for differentiated teaching in grades 3-5 / Sarah Bright and Katherine Kapustka.
Description: New York : Routledge, 2024. | Includes bibliographical references.
Identifiers: LCCN 2024028757 (print) | LCCN 2024028758 (ebook) | ISBN 9781032524320 (hardback) | ISBN 9781032520230 (paperback) | ISBN 9781003406662 (ebook)
Subjects: LCSH: Affective education—United States. | Individualized instruction—United States. | Gifted children—Education (Elementary)—Curricula—United States. | Language arts—Correlation with content subjects—United States. | Picture books for children—Educational aspects—United States.
Classification: LCC LB1072 .B75 2024 (print) | LCC LB1072 (ebook) | DDC 370.15/34—dc23/eng/20240822
LC record available at https://lccn.loc.gov/2024028757
LC ebook record available at https://lccn.loc.gov/2024028758

ISBN: 978-1-032-52432-0 (hbk)
ISBN: 978-1-032-52023-0 (pbk)
ISBN: 978-1-003-40666-2 (ebk)

DOI: 10.4324/9781003406662

Typeset in Palatino
by Apex CoVantage, LLC

Contents

Acknowledgments.. vi

Introduction... 1

1 Social and Emotional Learning Overview................ 6

2 Choosing Quality Books............................... 21

3 Matching Children to Books 41

4 Integrating SEL and Subject Content in
   Lesson Plans... 53

5 Integrating SEL and STEM............................. 71

6 Integrating SEL and Social Studies................... 95

7 Integrating SEL and ELA............................. 115

   Conclusion.. 143

Acknowledgments

While Sarah and Kathie's names are on the front cover, no book is written in isolation, and we are both thankful for the support and guidance we have received along the way.

We thank our local library systems for their book suggestions, and the use of their quiet workspaces when we needed to get out of our houses.

We thank the authors and illustrators who have created incredible graphic novels and illustrated texts that are works of art, inspirations, and fascinating sources of information for all ages.

We thank our colleagues and students at all of the educational institutions we have worked at over the last several decades. We have learned so much from you about learning and teaching.

And, most importantly, we thank our families, who mostly without complaint, have navigated piles of books left around the house and our focus on our writing, particularly in the last few weeks before our deadline.

Introduction

"How will I do it all?" In their work with pre-service teachers, this is a question that both Sarah and Kathie have encountered. For teachers in the upper elementary grades, standardized assessments are an ever-present concern, students have the unique social and emotional needs that accompany the beginnings of puberty, and for students who have struggled academically, the pressure to get them "caught up" may be intense. In many schools, teachers have learned that integration is a way to accomplish the myriad tasks that they are charged with completing during the limited school hours. Reading a text with social studies content in an English Language Arts (ELA) class is a way to address social studies standards, for example, and a narrative writing assignment can bring in aspects of social and emotional learning (SEL). We have designed this book to be one more support for teachers. It provides a framework to guide upper elementary teachers in integrating SEL with learning in the content areas and ELA, using diverse graphic novels and illustrated texts as the starting point.

A trip to the local bookstore, a glance around an elementary school library, or a review of the most recent "best of" lists for upper elementary students will reveal the explosion of graphic novels and other books that include a graphic component. In 2020, for example, *New Kid* by Jerry Craft was the first graphic novel to win the prestigious John Newbery Medal for distinguished contributions to American literature for children, and the Dog Man and Bad Guys series are immensely popular in some elementary schools. In addition, numerous picture books for older readers address complex topics and themes and provide an appropriate level of challenge as students develop and hone their literacy skills in the upper elementary grades. *Choosing Brave: How Mamie Till-Mobley and Emmett Till Sparked the Civil Rights Movement* by Angela Joy, for example, a 2023 Caldecott Honor Book, considers how Mami Till-Mobley turned her unimaginable grief into action after the murder of her 14-year-old son, Emmett Till.

Many teachers wish to reflect the range of diversities found in their classrooms and communities (e.g., ethnic, racial, cultural, linguistic, religious, socio-economic, familial, dis/ability, sexuality, and gender identity/expression) and authors and publishers are attuned to this focus. There are positive signs that children's books are becoming more diverse. Data from the Cooperative Children's Book Center at the University of Wisconsin-Madison, for example, shows that between 2015 and 2020, the number of books written by or featuring a BIPOC (Black, Indigenous, and person of color) character tripled, and that children's books revealing intersectional identifies, or aspects of identity other than race/ethnicity, are on the increase.

It is, however, a source of concern for us that since we submitted the manuscript for our first book in 2021, both SEL and children's literature have increasingly become controversial topics. While both of us adamantly oppose any effort to ban books, as educators and moms, we realize that not every book is appropriate for every child and that teachers often face a complex set of sometimes opposing responsibilities as they respect the expectations of their community while at the same time reflecting the diversities of the children in their classrooms and helping students to understand and empathize with people who are different. The books that we suggest in each of the chapters are books that we have reviewed, enjoyed, and can envision sharing with a group of upper elementary children. However, we are very aware of the challenges teachers face, and have written this book with the idea that teachers can use the framework and lessons as a starting point, and substitute books that meet their curricular needs, as well as the expectations of their communities.

Why These Books

We have chosen to focus on graphic novels and illustrated texts because we believe these "check all the boxes" for upper elementary students. For students who may struggle with reading or

English learners, pictures can support comprehension while providing students with well-written texts on topics that are of relevance and interest to students at this age (Senokossoff, 2013). The pictures also provide an opportunity for all students to analyze the message conveyed in both visuals and text, as they identify areas of congruity and incongruity between them. While some educators, parents, and even students themselves may be concerned that somehow these books are not "real" reading or that books with pictures are not appropriate, the wide range of adult graphic novels helps serve as a counterargument to this point, and the complex thought required to consider the intersection between texts and visuals can make for a more challenging reading task than reading a text alone.

In writing this book, we likely reviewed and considered hundreds of books to identify the ones that best served our purposes of being valuable both as exemplars for teaching in ELA and the content areas and as containing valuable social and emotional learning content. We have both gravitated towards books that contain a nuanced SEL message, rather than a "how to" approach, in addressing SEL challenges. As we considered books, we made a note of the ones that piqued our interest and that we could imagine sharing with our children, or with children in an upper elementary classroom. We also aimed to choose books which had characters representing the diversity of the communities in which we live and work. We are mindful that our readers work in different contexts, and we encourage you to find books that work with your students and communities.

Overview of the Book

Our goal with this book is to make educators' lives easier. We know that teachers work hard and are challenged with meeting the diverse academic and social and emotional needs of the children in their classroom as they align their teaching with content area standards, and, in many cases, prepare students for external accountability tests. This book provides concrete examples, including lesson ideas, book lists, and suggestions for differentiation, all of which are designed to give teachers a starting point that can be adapted to specific curricula and contexts.

The next three chapters of this book provide the research and theoretical foundation for understanding how and why to integrate content area and ELA learning with SEL, using graphic novels and illustrated texts as the basis for the lessons. Chapter 1 describes the main components of SEL, with specific consideration of the unique needs of upper elementary students. Chapter 2 focuses on understanding what makes graphic and illustrated texts unique, and how educators can identify quality books that will support the complex work that will be done in the lessons. Chapter 3 addresses the complexities of matching children to books, specifically considering some of the unique challenges teachers may face in the upper elementary grades, where the students' range of reading abilities may challenge teachers to find books that meet students' reading needs, are interesting and engaging, and also appropriate for the students' levels of maturity. The second section of the book, Chapters 4–7, focuses on specific techniques and examples for putting these ideas into practice in the classroom. Chapter 4 explains a framework for integrating SEL and content-area learning, and then Chapters 5–7 consider how to use these techniques in science, technology, engineering, math, social studies, and ELA with literary and informational texts. The book ends with a conclusion that provides a review of key concepts and encouragement to continue with this challenging work of designing truly integrated learning experiences that meet all learners' academic and SEL needs.

Notes to Our Readers

Throughout this book, we use the terms educators and teachers interchangeably. While we realize that most of our readers will be elementary teachers, or future teachers, we hope this book appeals to other school professionals, including administrators, librarians, counselors, and social workers, as well as those who work in more informal settings such as camps and after-school programs, and parents and caregivers who may be interested in supporting their children's academic and social and emotional development at home.

When referring to both authors and our collective best thinking, we will use the term *we*. If an experience applies to only one of us, we'll use our first names.

Throughout the book, we have chosen to use the Common Core State Standards and the national standards for science and social studies because of their broad reach within the United States. If your school or state uses other standards, we are confident you will see a significant overlap between the standards referenced in this book, and the topics, themes, and skills found in the standards relevant to your specific context.

Finally, as you read, do not hesitate to reach out to us. A quick internet search will help you find us regardless of where our professional journeys may lead us. We would love to hear what you think, how you are making sense of this book, and perhaps, most interesting for us, what you are reading!

References

Cooperative Children's Book Center. (2023, June 12). *CCBC's latest diversity statistics show increasing number of diverse books for children and teens* [Press release]. https://education.wisc.edu/news/ccbcs-latest-diversity-statistics-show-increasing-number-of-diverse-books-for-children-and-teens.

Senokossoff, G. W. (2013). Picture books are for little kids, aren't they? Using picture books with adolescent readers to enhance literacy instruction. *Reading Horizons: A Journal of Literacy and Language Arts*, 52(3). https://scholarworks.wmich.edu/reading_horizons/vol52/iss3/2

Book List

Blabey, A. (2016–2024). *Bad guys* (Vols. 1–19) (A. Blabey, Illus.). Scholastic Paperback.

Craft, J. (2019). *New kid*. Quill Tree Books.

Joy, A. (2022). *Choosing brave: How Mamie Till-Mobley and Emmett Till sparked the Civil Rights Movement* (J. Washington, Illus.). Roaring Book Press.

Pilkey, D. (2016–2024). *Dog man* (Vols. 1–12) (D. Pilkey, Illus.). Graphix.

1
Social and Emotional Learning Overview

In an undergraduate class I taught on children's literature, I asked my students what books from their childhood elicited powerful emotions—good or bad—and why. That question launched a rich and fascinating conversation about the feelings and lessons that students absorbed from their childhood and adolescent reading. I recently asked my own teenager to pose the same question to their friends, and I posted it on social media to compare answers from multiple generations. I received dozens of responses with a large range of book titles and reflections on why those books held special places in people's hearts and memories.

There were many classic books and series in people's lists: the Boxcar Children, Nancy Drew, the Hardy Boys, Winnie the Pooh, and the Little House on the Prairie series; and books by Judy Blume, Frances Hodgson Burnett, Beverly Clearly, Shel Silverstein, and E. B. White. The younger generation listed series including The Magic Treehouse, Harry Potter, Artemis Fowl, and Percy Jackson, along with individual books such as Neil Gaiman's *Blueberry Girl* and Audrey Wood's *King Bidgood's in the Bathtub*.

People remembered books because of the strong emotions they evoked. Some books brought feelings of comfort and joy: "*The Little Fur Family* because it made me feel warm and cozy amongst the wilds of the woods." Other books conjured up fear, sadness, and yearning. Several people held vivid memories of Katherine

Paterson's Newbery-winning novel *Bridge to Terabithia*, in which two children become friends and create a hidden magical kingdom that is accessible via a rope swing over a creek, which breaks and drops one of the children into the river, where she drowns. Other books that people cited that dealt with the deaths of beloved characters and other emotionally complex issues include Mildred Taylor's *Roll of Thunder, Hear My Cry*; Kenneth Thomasma's *Naya Nuki: Shoshoni Girl Who Ran*, Wilson Rawls' *Where the Red Fern Grows*, Jack London's *The Call of the Wild*, and *My Brother Sam is Dead*, by James Lincoln Collier and Christopher Collier.

Several friends remembered a sense of terror in connection with some of their most unforgettable childhood books, including Mordechai Richler's *Jacob Two-Two Meets the Hooded Fang*, a book of German fairy tales passed down through generations, and Rudyard Kipling's *Rikki-Tikki-Tavi* ("made me terrified of snakes"). One friend told me, "My Grade 7 teacher read us Robert C. O'Brien's *Z for Zachariah*, a little bit each day for weeks upon weeks of nightmares for the whole class."

A teacher and mother of two teenaged girls named *A Taste of Blackberries* by Doris Buchanan Smith as a book that has stuck with her:

> It was one of the books on the 5th grade reading list. It was a long list, we got to choose the ones we wanted. I ended up reading all but two. This is the only book I remember. I was traumatized by the death of the kid by an allergic reaction. I still think about this book, especially having a kid with a food allergy . . ..

These memorable books taught students how to identify and process their emotions, and to better understand the world and their place in it. My closest childhood friend listed a few books that stand out in her memory and explained why:

> Daniel Pinkwater's *The Big Orange Splot* because it showed differences as good; Judith Voigt's *Alexander & the Terrible, Horrible, No Good Very Bad Day* for normalizing grumpiness and showing you can turn it around; the Frog & Toad

books for the characters (mostly Toad); William Steig's *Sylvester and the Magic Pebble* for the illustrations and the devoted parents.

The children's librarian in our local public library saw herself in another world through one of her most memorable books:

> I loved the "B Is for Betsy" books by Carolyn Haywood. I was a poor kid, in tract housing and toughskin jeans who really wanted to wear dresses and red ribbons in my hair. I wanted my mom waiting at home in a dress with a snack and Officer Kirkpatrick to give a tug on my braid as he helped me across the street.

The lessons and emotions that these books imparted were all facets of social and emotional learning (SEL), the process of helping to build healthy self-concepts, manage relationships and conflicts, and develop skills to navigate challenges in personal, social, and academic situations. SEL is vital to children's development from the earliest age. Educators, mental health professionals, community and family members, and others in child support roles use SEL to foster the skills that children need to navigate challenging situations, both in school and in life outside the classroom.

In this chapter we will provide a definition of SEL and give an overview of the most cited SEL framework in K-12 schools. We will summarize research on the use and effectiveness of SEL programs in the school setting and discuss ways to support SEL in elementary schools. We will conclude with an explanation of the use of graphic novels and other illustrated texts to support students socially and emotionally within an academic setting, guiding students as they make meaningful connections between their culture, languages, and lived experiences.

What is Social and Emotional Learning?

Social and emotional learning (SEL) comprises three parts: social SEL skills, emotional SEL skills, and cognitive SEL skills. Social

SEL skills help students understand and respond to challenging social situations and interpersonal conflicts, work cooperatively, and demonstrate positive emotions such as kindness and empathy toward others. Emotional SEL skills allow students to develop emotional intelligence, which helps them to understand and navigate their own emotions and recognize and appropriately respond to other people's feelings and points of view. Cognitive SEL skills include executive functioning abilities, such as planning, prioritization and completion of tasks, working memory, self-regulation and inhibitory control, and flexibility (Cramer & Castro-Olivo, 2016; Hamilton & Doss, 2020).

SEL has a positive impact at three levels: internal, interpersonal, and societal or global. At the individual level, SEL fosters internal growth, stability, and maturity in such ways as helping children manage and express their emotions. Interpersonally, SEL supports relationship skills, such as good communication, conflict management, and problem solving. At the societal or global level, SEL tools help people learn how to be a global citizen who builds and contributes positively to the world—socially, economically, politically, and environmentally.

Each SEL skill or competency has developmentally appropriate milestones that build on one another and become more focused at higher grades (Jones et al., 2017). For example, social skills for younger children include understanding and communicating emotions, which is necessary for children's interactions beginning at the earliest ages. By middle and high school, navigating and communicating emotions is a highly complex process wrapped up in adolescent physical, social, and academic challenges.

Numerous large-scale, longitudinal studies completed since the introduction of SEL programs in the 1990s have proven the positive impact of SEL on a wide array of children's social-emotional skills, classroom behavior, and attitudes, and well-being indicators such as a stable self-concept and stress management (Green et al., 2021; Taylor et al., 2017). A review of 523 studies of SEL programs that were conducted in 24 countries with over 1 million students found that SEL programs have "consistent, positive impacts on a broad range of student outcomes including increased SEL skills, attitudes, prosocial behaviors, and academic achievement and decreased conduct problems and emotional distress" (Durlak et al., 2022, p. 765). Additional reviews of the research found long-term benefits for students: those who participated in SEL programs had an 11-percentile point gain in long-term achievement over students who did not participate in SEL programs (Mahoney, 2018), and a Brookings Institute study found that SEL programming can have a positive impact for up to 18 years on academic achievement, social competence, conduct problems, emotional distress, and drug use (CASEL, n.d.; Cefai et al., 2022; Durlak & Mahoney, 2019; Wigelsworth et al., 2022).

Frameworks for SEL

An analysis by the American Institutes for Research found 136 SEL frameworks for ages 6–25 that examined more than 20 areas of study, including school-based competency development, mindfulness, resilience, and public health (Berg et al., 2017). Harvard University's Explore SEL project offers a Framework Profiles tool that compares SEL frameworks by such criteria as age range of the students, setting (schools, home, or other), developer type (government, non-profit, research, and school-based), language, and region.

Harvard University's Explore SEL project maintains an online database of more than 40 widely adopted SEL frameworks in a variety of disciplines. The Explore SEL project uses six domains of SEL to categorize the frameworks:

- **Cognitive**, which includes developing executive functioning skills such as goal setting, task initiation, and time management; good decision-making; problem-solving and working through challenges; and learning from failure
- **Emotion**, which includes the understanding, expression, and control of students' own emotions, and the interpretation and appropriate responses to other children's emotions

- **Social**, which includes communicating, playing, and interacting with others, and understanding and managing conflicts in a healthy way
- **Values**, which include the development of ethical values, character traits, and habits that position a child to be a compassionate person who contributes to their community and world in positive ways
- **Perspectives**, which include nurturing such outlooks as optimism, courage, gratitude, and hope; developing a growth mindset, grit, and perseverance; expanding self-confidence and willingness to step outside comfort zones; and welcoming mentoring to grow from critiques and criticism
- **Identity**, which includes building a healthy self-awareness, self-efficacy, and sense of identity and place in the world, and fostering an understanding of the diversity of identities within local and global communities

These six domains cover aspects of social and emotional competencies and skills from broad categories such as core academic skills to specific traits such as flexibility and stress tolerance. The Explore SEL website (http://exploresel.gse.harvard.edu), which is regularly updated to include new frameworks, also includes a Framework Profiles tool that allows users to compare frameworks across multiple domains to show the commonalities and differences between the frameworks.

The most commonly cited framework is the framework from the Collaborative for Academic, Social, and Emotional Learning (CASEL), which includes five key SEL competencies: 1) self-awareness (understanding the impact of emotions and action); 2) self-management (managing emotions and behavior); 3) social awareness (understanding the perspectives and circumstances of other people and institutions); 4) relationship skills (establishing healthy and supportive relationships); and 5) responsible decision-making (CASEL, 2020). The CASEL framework (Figure 1.1) shows four areas of implementation: in the classroom, where SEL can be embedded in the curriculum and in the climate of the classroom; in schools, where administrators implement consistent policies and support in all areas; by families and caregivers; and in the communities through aligned learning opportunities with schools and families. The coordination of all four areas of SEL implementation helps to ensure an inclusive culture and consistent application of the SEL policies (Mahoney et al., 2020).

The CASEL framework provides a picture of the skills, abilities, mindsets, and outlooks that comprise a fully realized and participating individual in our society—one who is aware of their views and impacts and their responsibilities within their community and the world as a whole.

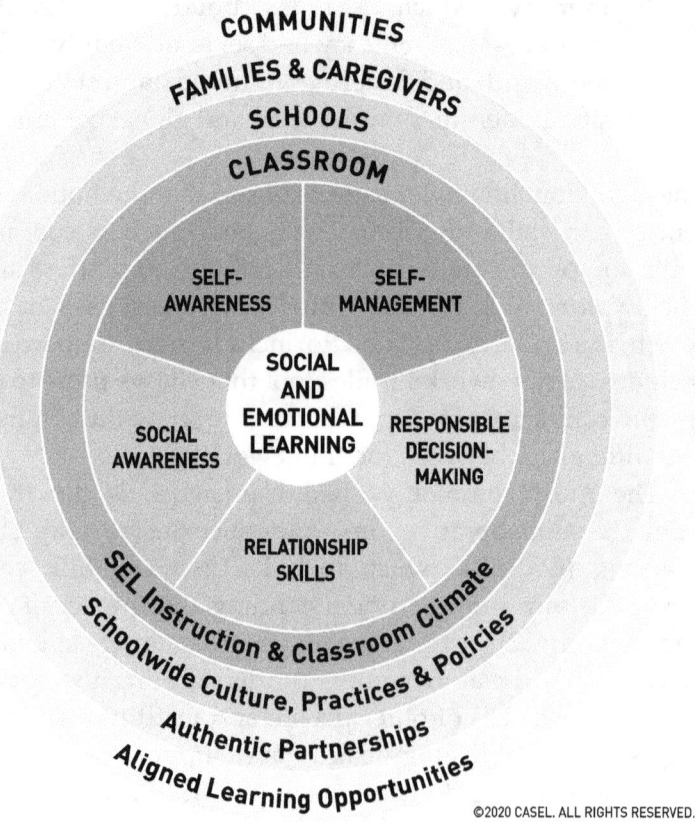

FIGURE 1.1 The CASEL Wheel of Social and Emotional Learning
Source: © 2024 CASEL. All rights reserved. https://casel.org/fundamentals-of-sel/what-is-the-casel-framework.

Implementing SEL Programs in Schools and Classrooms

Although there are no national SEL standards, all 50 states now include SEL competencies within their PreK-12 standards, with 15 states having adopted SEL competencies since 2020 (Stanford & Meisner, 2023). Though the specific emphases differ among SEL standards and frameworks, the most common overarching recommendations for K-12 SEL standards are that the SEL content and pedagogy should be differentiated, inclusive, and presented repeatedly in multiple contexts throughout the students' learning experiences (APA, 2017). A limitation to many SEL programs is that they are administered as single, stand-alone lessons given once a week or less. Such small doses of SEL instruction have limited effect because SEL skills, like academic skills, develop over time and require continuous implementation in multiple settings (Jones & Bouffard, 2012).

CASEL recommends that the content and pedagogy of the SEL programs be customized for the cognitive, emotional, and social needs of the students, and states that the programs should be adjusted over time to fit the children's changing developmental abilities and needs (Jones et al., 2017). In 2020, CASEL updated aspects of its definition and framework SEL programs "to pay close attention to how SEL affirms the identities, strengths and experiences of all children, including those who have been marginalized in our education systems" (Niemi, 2020). The Education Collaboratory at Yale University's School of Medicine's 2024 news brief on SEL stated that research and practice around SEL has not focused on marginalized student identities, a failing that must be corrected by the inclusion and relevance of SEL materials to all children's cultural, linguistic, socioeconomic, gender, and sexual identities so that all students feel engaged, empowered, and included (Osuoha, 2024). Such concepts as ability, self-concept, and happiness and well-being should be presented within students' specific cultural contexts, and those contexts should be shared universally, fostering understanding and empathy among students. The recommendations for lessons and books provided in this book are aimed at providing support for a diverse range of students, to address that shortcoming.

SEL Applications and Programs in Upper Elementary Grades

As with any curriculum, the expectations and outcomes for SEL vary depending on the children's age, grade, and ability level. The CASEL framework does not provide grade-level performance indicators or competencies, but many organizations have taken the CASEL framework to create grade-level learning, benchmarks, and performance descriptors. Dusenbury et al. (2015) list two key SEL competences for the elementary grades: students should be able to independently negotiate and manage peer relationships, friendships, and conflicts; and students should be able to demonstrate appropriate emotions in a variety of contexts. The state of Illinois, for example, created three SEL goals with performance descriptors and benchmarks at five grade-level clusters. Their three SEL goals, which share key concepts with the CASEL competencies, are: 1) develop self-awareness and self-management skills to achieve school and life success; 2) use social-awareness and interpersonal skills to establish and maintain positive relationships; and 3) demonstrate decision-making skills and responsible behaviors in personal, school, and community contexts. At the upper elementary grades the performance descriptors include having children "describe a range of emotions and the situations that cause them" and "describe and demonstrate ways to express emotions in a socially acceptable manner"; "identify differences among and contributions of various social and cultural groups" and "demonstrate how to work effectively with those who are different from oneself"; and "describe causes and consequences of conflicts" and "apply constructive approaches in resolving conflicts" (Illinois State Board of Education, n.d.).

To take a specific example of implementation, CASEL launched the Collaborating States Initiative to help state education agencies facilitate the promotion of SEL. As a result of this initiative, CASEL published a *Theory of Action* (Yoder et al., 2021), which defines SEL and presents a state-level *Theory of Action* that provides instructions on how to use the tool. A downloadable rubric, available on the CASEL site, helps schools plan the steps that are needed to reach the goals of each focus area. Under Focus area 1A, Build Awareness, Commitment, and Ownership, there are three steps to be taken: 1) build an SEL team; 2) provide foundational SEL learning opportunities; and 3) build two-way communication between the SEL team and all stakeholders, such as staff, community partners, families, and other caregivers.

Using Illustrated Texts to Teach SEL in Elementary Grades

Tools such as CASEL's *Theory of Action* help administrators implement SEL systems in schools and help educators build lessons and curricular materials to support SEL in the classroom. At the classroom level, the integration of books with content lessons is an excellent way to incorporate SEL themes and lessons. Graphic novels and illustrated texts offer many lenses through which children can see themselves and others in the books' characters, plots, and themes. Books use stories, illustrations, and dialogue to show kindness and compassion, demonstrate problem-solving, display communication challenges, illustrate conflicts and their management and resolution, and present wise and poor decision-making. The integration of books with SEL lessons helps educators address a variety of social and emotional lessons and challenges, empowering children to develop healthy motivation and engagement, high self-esteem, strong communication and interpersonal relations, and a strong and healthy self-concept (Halsted, 2009; Lamont, 2012).

Illustrated texts can be the foundation for a lesson plan that teaches, comforts, supports, and builds connections with and among students. Books can also provide the structure for a differentiated lesson by engaging students at various reading levels and on topics that are related but offer different perspectives through their characters, plot, and images. A lesson plan that uses books to teach SEL skills would typically have four components. The first is group reading of the book and a reflection immediately afterwards that touches on the themes in it and the actions and feelings of the characters, relating them back to how the students responded to the text. A second component is a group activity that reflects the lessons and values of the texts, such as discussion, role-playing, story-telling or reenactment, art activities, or journaling and other writing activities (Hébert & Furner, 1997; Hynes-Berry, 2012).

The third stage of an SEL lesson plan includes differentiated individual or small-group activities that are customized for the ability levels and interests of the students. At this stage, students could read books on the same topic but at different reading levels. The activities could include choice boards with options ranging from fairly simple recall assignments to more complex analytical exercises, as well as small-group activities involving research and a presentation on a topic related to the book. Examples of projects include paper-based assignments, such as a multi-paneled graphic story, a piece of art, or a printed newspaper, newsletter, flier, or poster that could be posted or distributed in the school. Digital projects include a PowerPoint or Google Slides presentation, a blog post or web page, an online newspaper, and a piece of digital art.

The fourth and final component of the lesson is closure and reflection, in which the students come together and share and discuss their findings. This is an opportunity for students to look back at the introductory discussion or activity that began the lesson, share the work that they did alone or in small groups and discuss similarities and differences among their projects, and then discuss the lesson. By pulling together the similarities and differences in the students' materials, projects, and viewpoints, the lesson introduces students to new and different perspectives while supporting students at different levels as they study and understand the topic.

Each lesson can teach individual SEL competencies or multiple domains, depending on the focus of the lesson, the age of the students, and the content used. For example, a lesson about conflict management would draw on recognizing and sharing emotions, making good decisions, and communicating clearly. The books can be subject-specific, focusing on such topics as language arts, social studies, and science. and incorporating relevant standards and cross-curricular, linking themes across multiple subjects, such as social studies and science, language arts and science, or art and science.

In Chapters 2 and 3, we will illustrate how to identify quality illustrated texts and discuss the factors teachers need to take into consideration when choosing books for classroom or small-group settings, including students' interests, reading ability levels, and content comprehension levels. The later chapters will consider how to address SEL in the specific content areas of science, social studies, and English Language Arts (ELA).

References

American Psychological Association (APA), Center for Psychology in Schools and Education. (2017). *Top 20 principles from psychology for preK–12 creative, talented, and gifted students' teaching and learning.* www.apa.org/ed/schools/teaching-learning/top-twenty-principles.aspx

Berg, J., Osher, D., Same, M. R., Nolan, E., Benson, D., & Jacobs, N. (2017). *Identifying, defining, and measuring social and emotional competencies.* American Institutes for Research.

CASEL. (n.d.). *CASEL: History.* https://casel.org/history

CASEL. (2020). *CASEL'S SEL Framework: What are the core competence areas and where are they promoted?* www.casel.org/what-is-SEL

Cefai, C., Camilleri, L., Bartolo, P., Grazzani, I., Cavioni, V., Conte, E., Ornaghi, V., Agliati, A., Gandellini, S., Tatalovic Vorkapic, S., Poulou, M., Martinsone, B., Stokenberga, I., Simões, C., Santos, M., & Colomeischi, A. A. (2022). The effectiveness of a school-based, universal mental health programme in six European countries. *Frontiers in Psychology, 13*(925614): 1–13. https://doi.org/10.3389/fpsyg.2022.925614

Cramer, K. M. & Castro-Olivo, S. (2016). Effects of a culturally adapted social-emotional learning intervention program on students' mental health. *Contemporary School Psychology, 20*(2): 118–129.

Durlak, J. A. & Mahoney, J. L. (2019). *The practical benefits of an SEL program.* CASEL.

Durlak, J. A., Mahoney, J. L., & Boyle, A. E. (2022). What we know, and what we need to find out about universal, school-based social and emotional learning programs for children and adolescents: A review of meta-analyses and directions for future research. *Psychological Bulletin, 148*(11–12): 765–782. https://doi.org/10.1037/bul0000383

Dusenbury, L., Calin, S., Domitrovich, S., & Weissberg, R. P. (2015). *What does evidence-based instruction in social and emotional learning actually look like in practice? Evidence-based instruction in social and emotional learning. A brief on findings from CASEL's Program Reviews.* CASEL. https://eric.ed.gov/?id=ED574862#:~:text=One%20approach%20uses%20free%2Dstanding,and%20emotional%20development%20in%20students

Green, A. L., Ferrante, S., Boaz, T. L., Kutash, K., & Wheeldon-Reece, B. (2021). Social and emotional learning during early adolescence: Effectiveness of a classroom-based SEL program for middle school students. *Psychology in the Schools, 58*(6): 1056–1069. https://doi.org/10.1002/pits.22487

Halsted, J. W. (2009). *Some of my best friends are books: Guiding gifted readers from preschool to high school.* Great Potential Press, Inc.

Hamilton, L. S. & Doss, C. J. (2020). *Supports for social and emotional learning in schools: Findings from the American Teacher Panel.* RAND Corporation.

Hébert, T. P. & Furner, J. M. (1997). Helping high ability students overcome math anxiety through bibliotherapy. *Journal of Secondary Gifted Education, 8*(4): 164–178.

Hynes-Berry, M. (2012). *Don't leave the story in the book: Using literature to guide inquiry in early childhood classrooms.* Teachers College Press.

Illinois State Board of Education. (n.d.). *Social-emotional learning standards.* https://www.isbe.net/Documents/SEL-Standards.pdf

Jones, S. M. & Bouffard, S. M. (2012). Social policy report: Social and emotional learning in schools from programs to strategies. *Sharing Child and Youth Development Knowledge 26*(4): 1–33.

Jones, S. M., Barnes, S. P., Bailey, R., & Doolittle E. J. (2017). Promoting social and emotional competencies in elementary school. *The Future of Children, 27*(1): 49–72.

Lamont, R. T. (2012). The fears and anxieties of gifted learners: Tips for parents and educators. *Gifted Child Today, 35*(4): 271–276.

Mahoney, J. L. (2018, November 26). *An update on social and emotional learning outcome research.* kappanonline.org. https://kappanonline.org/social-emotional-learning-outcome-research-mahoney-durlak-weissberg

Mahoney, J. L., Weissberg, R. P., Greenberg, M. T., Dusenbury, L., Jagers, R. J., Niemi, K., Schlinger, M., Schlund, J., Shriver, T. P., & VanAusdal, K. (2020). Systemic social and emotional learning: Promoting educational success for all preschool to high school students. *American Psychologist 76*(7): 1128–1142.

Niemi, K. (2020, December 15). *Niemi: CASEL is updating the most widely recognized definition of social-emotional learning. Here's why.* https://www.the74million.org/article/niemi-casel-is-updating-the-most-widely-recognized-definition-of-social-emotional-learning-heres-why

Osuoha, E. (2024, March 1). *Advancing SEL science & practice: The Education Collaboratory & #SELDay*. Retrieved April 9, 2024, from https://medicine.yale.edu/news-article/selday

Stanford, L. & Meisner, C. (2023, July 27). Social-emotional learning persists despite political backlash. *Education Week*. https://www.edweek.org/leadership/social-emotional-learning-persists-despite-political-backlash/2023/07

Taylor, R. D., Oberle, E., Durlak, J. A., & Weissberg, R. P. (2017). Promoting positive youth development through school-based social and emotional learning interventions: A meta-analysis of follow-up effects. *Child Development, 88*(4): 1156–1171.

Wigelsworth, M., Verity, L., Mason, C., Qualter, P., & Humphrey, N. (2022). Social and emotional learning in primary schools: A review of the current state of evidence. *British Journal of Educational Psychology, 92*(3): 898–924. https://doi.org/10.1111/bjep.12480

Yoder, N., Martinez-Black, T., Dermody, C., Godek, D., & Dusenbury, L. (2021). Theory of action: Systemic social and emotional learning for states. CASEL. https://casel.org/systemic-social-and-emotional-learning-for-states

Book List

Brown, M. W. (1946). *The little fur family* (G. Williams, Illus.). Harper & Brothers.

Colfer, E. O. (2001–2021). *Artemis Fowl* (Vols. 1–11). Penguin.

Collier, J. L. & Collier, C. (1974). *My brother Sam is dead*. Scholastic.

Dixon, F. W. (1927–1958). *The Hardy boys mystery stories* (Vols. 1–58). Grosset & Dunlap.

Gaiman, N. (2008). *Blueberry Girl* (C. Vess, Illus.). HarperCollins.

Haywood, C. (1939–1977). *"B" is for Betsy* (Vols. 1–12). Harcourt, Brace, & World.

Keene, C. (1930–1979). *The Nancy Drew mystery stories* (Vols. 1–56). Grosset & Dunlap.

Kipling, R. (1894). Riki Tiki Tavi. In *The Jungle Book* (J. L. Kipling, Illus.). Macmillan.

Lobel, A. (1970–1979). *Frog and Toad* (Vols. 1–4) (A. Lobel, Illus.). Harper & Row.

London, J. (1903). *The call of the wild* (P. R. Goodwin & C. L. Bull, Illus.). Macmillan.

Milne, A. A. (1926–1927). *Winnie the Pooh* (Vols. 1–4) (E. H. Shepard, Illus.). Dutton Books

O'Brien, R. C. (1974). *Z for Zachariah*. G. K. Hall.

Osborne, M. P. (1992–2024). *The magic treehouse* (Vols. 1–39) (S. Murdocca, Illus.). Random House.

Paterson, K. (1977). *The bridge to Terabithia* (D. Diamond, Illus.). Thomas Y. Crowell Co.

Pinkwater, D. M. (1977). *The big orange splot* (D. M. Pinkwater, Illus.). Scholastic.

Rawls, W. (1961). *Where the red fern grows*. Doubleday.

Richler, M. (1975). *Jacob Two-Two meets the Hooded Fang*. McClelland & Stewart.

Riordan, R. (2005–2023). *Percy Jackson and the Olympian* (Vols. 1–6). Disney Hyperion.

Rowling, J. K. (1997–2007). *Harry Potter* (Vols. 1–7). Scholastic.

Smith, D. B. (1973). *A taste of blackberries*. Thomas C. Crowell Co,

Steig, W. (1969). *Sylvester and the magic pebble* (W. Steig, Illus.). Simon & Schuster.

Taylor, M. D. (1977). *Roll of thunder, hear my cry*. Dial Press.

Thomasma, K. (1983). *Naya Nuki: Shoshoni girl who ran* (E. Hundley, Illus.). Baker Books.

Voight, J. (1972). *Alexander and the terrible, horrible, no good, very bad day* (R. Cruz, Illus.). Atheneum Books.

Warner, G. C. (1924–1976). *The boxcar children* (Vols. 1–19). Rand McNally.

2

Choosing Quality Books

With so many graphic novels and illustrated texts being published each year, with varying quality, themes, topics, and characters, the search for the "just right" book to put in the hands of young people can be daunting. As educators, we want the books to be both educative and enjoyable for students, because we know that students are more likely to read, and to continue reading, when they are engaged with the text. Additionally, as students get older, and connections with peers become more important, reading the "it" book so that they can join in the social aspects of sharing a book can be a motivating factor. Kathie and Sarah are both of an age where they can remember putting their names down on a paper list at the library to get the latest Beverly Cleary book, and despairing when they saw how far down the list their names were. Those lists have been replaced by today's "holds" on books by authors such as Raina Telgemeier and Jeff Kinney, but the connections to texts and the social aspects of reading are no less important.

As educators, we also know that books have the power to unite a class around a shared literacy experience For Kathie, reading *Stone Fox* to her class and watching as her fifth-grade students, just on the cusp of adolescence, allowed themselves to be vulnerable with their feelings in front of their peers is a powerful memory. As a teacher educator, Kathie often asks her students in literacy methods courses to identify a text that was particularly powerful when they were in upper elementary school. While the book titles vary, several themes are commonly mentioned. Some students identify a book that was powerful because of who they shared it with (e.g., friends, teachers, or parents), others remember a book that helped them find joy in reading for the first time, and still others reference books they connected to in a more mature way, perhaps a book that addressed a difficult topic or issue in a way that made sense to them as an upper elementary student. While you read this chapter, you might think about the books that come to mind when you remember your time in the upper elementary grades, or perhaps those you are reading with the students in your classroom now. When you remember a book, take a moment to consider why, of all the books you have read both before and since, that particular text holds a place in your mind. As we provide suggestions for how to identify and choose quality graphic novels and illustrated texts to support learning in the content areas, literacy, and SEL, reflecting on the books that "mattered" and the reasons for your connections to them will help you create a frame for understanding which books you want to give a privileged place in your lessons.

Chapter 1 provided a comprehensive overview of the SEL needs of upper elementary students. Building on that foundation, this chapter provides guidance on how to choose the graphic texts that will best support integrating SEL in the teaching of the content areas and ELA. First, we will explain the scope of graphic texts, followed by the unique qualities of these texts that make them not just appropriate for older readers, but a source for both challenge and engagement. Then we'll provide resources and suggestions for identifying the quality books that you will want to include in your lessons. Finally, the chapter will conclude with a consideration of the specific ways these texts can be of value as educators work to integrate SEL with teaching in the content areas and ELA.

What are Graphic Texts and Why Should We Use Them?

As literacy educators, we struggled with the appropriate term to use to explain the scope of the books we were using in this text. We considered a variety of terms with the words "picture" and "graphic" in them. For example, the term "picture book" is defined by the American Library Association as a book that provides a visual experience for the reader where pictures provide support for the story, theme, or concept (ALA, 2023). While not excluded from the category of "picture book" by the definition, in common parlance, graphic novels and other books that use a comic format are not usually considered "picture" books, even though these books use pictures to convey meaning. To add another level of complexity, the term graphic novel is often used to refer to both fiction and non-fiction texts, although the term novel usually refers to a work of fiction. The American Library Association Graphic Novels and Comics Round Table defines graphic novels as "trade compilations and original works published in the sequential art format with an overarching story and/or theme" (ALA Graphic Novels and Comics Round Table, 2023). Within this book, we will refer to "graphic novels and illustrated texts" as an umbrella term for both traditional picture books and graphic "novels" both of which include literary and informational texts.

From a reader's perspective, an illustrated text or graphic novel is likely to be distinguished quickly from a traditional chapter book by the prominence of the visuals. However, the importance of these visuals goes beyond the number and placement. While some chapter books may include a few pictures, often at the beginning of each chapter, these pictures act as a supplement to, rather than an essential component of, the text. In graphic novels and illustrated texts, visuals play an important role in telling the story or conveying information and thus are an essential component of the overall text. Additionally, because graphic novels and illustrated books usually have fewer words than chapter books, each word must be chosen with care. As a thought experiment, or perhaps an introductory activity to do with your students, consider reading either only the pictures or only the text of a traditional chapter book with limited pictures. You will likely get none of the meaning from just the pictures, and not miss the visual component if you only read the text. For graphic novels and many illustrated texts, you will likely need both to get the full meaning and experience from the book. These texts are unique because they combine text and visuals to create a whole that is greater than its parts.

The power of these texts lies in their multimodality, or communicating in more than one "mode." For learners growing up in a digital age, multimodality is the norm. Websites, magazine and newspaper articles, as well as informational and literary texts all require readers to take in information from words and images to make meaning, because "the words and pictures transact with each other, and transform each other (Sipe, 1998, p. 98). This adds to the complexity for readers. Unlike emergent readers who may rely on pictures to support their identification of words and their comprehension, most older readers of graphic texts do not "need" the pictures for basic word identification, but the pictures are an essential part of the experience when reading graphic novels and illustrated texts. Particularly in graphic novels, the pictures may tell more of the story than the words, as key elements like characters' emotions, settings, and time changes may be portrayed in pictures, but not stated in the text. For this reason, particularly with graphic novels, it is important to teach students to read the pictures as much as they read the words (Smith & Pole, 2018). Most commonly in books, the pictures and texts are telling the same story (congruency) but at times, there is a deviation between what the words say and what the pictures show. *A Couple of Boys Have the Best Week Ever* by Marla Frazee is a good example of deviation. As the boys head off to camp, the text states that one of the boys only packed a few belongings, but the picture behind him shows a mountain of boxes, bags, and baskets. Another example is the popular text *I Want My Hat Back* by Jon Klaussen. In this book, a bear asks the rabbit if he has seen his hat. The rabbit has the hat on his head, but he denies that he has seen it, and the bear continues on his search. These examples of deviation often add humor to the story because the readers either feel like they are being let in on an inside joke or they realize something the character does not. In either case, deviation or congruency, the power of graphic novels and illustrated texts is in "the union of text and art that results in something beyond what each form separately contributes" (Wolfenberger & Sipe, 2007, p. 273).

Whether a text is a more traditional picture book for older readers or a graphic novel that conveys meaning through picture panels and more limited text, these books are also unique because they rely upon different cognitive structures, those required for attending to verbal input, and those required for analyzing visual information (Sipe, 1998). These two different forms of information also influence how readers interact with graphic novels and illustrated texts. The verbal information leads the reader to read linearly, to not interrupt the flow of the reading, while the visual information encourages the reader to stop reading and to attend to the unique features of the images. Ideally, older, proficient readers will be taught to read these books differently than, perhaps, the way they read a traditional chapter book. They may pause and move forward and backward in the book, or even read the book multiple times to get a full grasp of the material presented (McClanahan & Nottingham, 2019). Full comprehension of the story will require that students are taught to consider all aspects of the visual design, including line, shape, color, orientation, symbols, framing, and point of view (Serafini, 2014).

The understanding that reading is a complex process that requires attending to the interplay of words and visuals is supported by a review of the Common Core State Standards for English Language Arts. Anchor Standard 7, which applies to both informational and literary texts, states that students should be able to: "integrate and evaluate content presented in diverse media and formats, including visually and quantitatively, as well as in words" (NGACBP & CCSSO, 2010, p. 10). In fourth grade, for example, students reading informational texts are expected to note how the information presented in visuals contributes to the overall understanding of the text, and, in fifth grade, readers of literature are expected to explain how visual or multimedia elements "contribute to the meaning, tone, or beauty of the text" (p. 12). In addition to these standards which focus on reading, within the Common Core ELA standards, there are also standards related to the analysis of visual and multimedia elements in Writing and Speaking and Listening. In Writing, the section of anchor standards that focuses on acquiring and presenting knowledge includes using print and digital media and literary and informational text, all of which include both texts and visuals. In Speaking and Listening, Anchor Standard 2 asks students to: "Integrate and evaluate information presented in diverse media and formats, including visually, quantitatively, and orally" (NGACBP & CCSSO, 2010, p. 22). These connections demonstrate what teachers likely already know: with guidance from a teacher, graphic novels and illustrated texts provide a unique cognitive challenge, address the learning standards that students must attain to be seen as fully literate in the 21st century, and are often engaging texts that children will want to read.

As students get older, there might be a tendency to move away from the use of graphic novels and illustrated texts as important components of instruction, and perhaps a move to encourage students to read more traditional chapter books. For numerous reasons, this would be a mistake. On a purely practical level, these books are readily available in school and public libraries as well as through digital platforms. They cover a variety of topics and themes at numerous different reading and content complexity levels. This is particularly important when considering how to meet the unique academic needs of students in upper elementary grades because books at different levels focused on a common topic or theme can be chosen to meet the needs of all readers found in a classroom.

While embodying the unique and intellectually challenging features defined above, illustrated texts for older readers and graphic novels also provide a level of comfort that may be helpful as students transition from the picture books that dominated their early literacy experiences to the more text-heavy books that are likely to be common in middle and high school classrooms. Teachers may notice that some children go through a phase where they gravitate toward graphic texts as they "grow out of" easier traditional picture books, but before they are fully comfortable with chapter books. It is also important to note that picture books with topics, themes, and vocabulary for older readers should also play a role in upper elementary classrooms, even if students are reading proficiently. These texts, which are often short enough to read in one class period, can serve as "anchor texts" for learning a variety of skills and strategies including those related to understanding and analyzing the interplay between text and visual images, provide a shared experience for discussion, and introduce new topics and ideas.

Particularly in the upper elementary grades, as the content demands in science and social studies become more intense, illustrated texts can be valuable for read-alouds. Graphic-format texts are less often used for whole-class instruction because they are not meant to be read aloud, although, using modern technology such as a document camera, they can be shared with a whole class. Illustrated books, however, can serve as an introduction to a topic, or provide an in-depth look at one aspect of the unit of study, particularly at a time when curricula in science and social studies can be criticized for their surface-level coverage of many topics. As Serafini (2011) states, a well-chosen book in a content area lesson "brings the topics under consideration to life and demonstrates how literature is a way of knowing the world in which we live, as well as an avenue of escape into other worlds" (p. 32). A biography of a particular figure in history or of a scientist can help students make deep connections to the subject, or to see the human side of a particular historical event. It is one thing to read about the Civil War in a history textbook, but learning about an unsung hero, George Scott, the fugitive enslaved person whose actions helped save a Union fort and led to the end of slavery, by reading *Seeking Freedom: The Untold Story of Fortress Monroe and the Ending of Slavery in America* by Selene Castrovilla, is a very different experience.

What Makes a Good Text for Children?

Perhaps it goes without saying, but rather than beginning with a list of specific considerations that you will want to bear in mind as you identify the texts you want to use in your classroom, the most important characteristic is your enthusiasm for a book (Weih, 2015). If the book does not impress us, or engage us in a unique way, how can we expect it to engage our students? Of course, a "good" book can be good for many different reasons;

it can be good because it matches the content, skill, or SEL competency we are teaching, or because it represents our students in a powerful way, or simply because it is a book that provoked an emotional reaction. The somewhat challenging task for educators is to identify the books that are both engaging to us and our students and also support the educational goals.

Initial Considerations

Finding the best book for any given lesson is a bit like a scavenger hunt, and while there are many good books available that address the topics and themes that are taught in upper elementary classrooms, it may be difficult to find one book that meets all of our needs and expectations. A book, for example, might meet the content or ELA standard and have a strong SEL connection, but it might not reflect the diversity of the classroom or the broader community. Alternatively, maybe the book has strong SEL connections and shows a variety of diverse experiences, but the connections to the content or ELA standards might not be as strong as we would like. Because it is sometimes not possible to find one book that meets all of our needs, it can be helpful to look at the total "text diet" for students throughout a unit or a school year. Over a broad period of time, a teacher can make sure that the books are addressing the academic and social and emotional needs of the students, as well as the need to both be "seen" in books, and encounter the full scope of diversity in the wider world.

As students enter the upper elementary grades, they can also take part in interrogating the texts that they encounter. This promotes the critical literacy skills that students will need as they are exposed to multiple types of media and are asked to consider the perspectives presented. In the upper elementary grades, students are capable of asking whose perspectives are present and whose are missing. Who is visible in this book and who is absent? Who are the authors, and what is their background or expertise in the information or experiences presented? Organizations such as We Need Diverse Books focus on diversifying all aspects of the children's book publishing realm, by supporting diverse authors, illustrators, and publishing professionals toward the goal of making sure that all children can see themselves represented in the books they encounter. The goal of this movement is not to prevent authors from choosing to write about topics of interest, but rather highlight and support authors and illustrators who share the same characteristics (e.g., race, class, gender, language, dis/ability, sexual orientation) as the individuals or characters in the books they produce (Rodriguez et al., 2020).

Students are also continuing to develop metacognitive abilities, and their increasing knowledge of the world beyond their family, school, and community makes it a perfect time for students to draw connections (Harvey & Goudvis, 2017; Keene & Zimmerman (2007) as well as disconnections to what they read. It can be equally empowering for students to see themselves in the text, but also to be able to articulate when the lived experiences of the characters or individuals are significantly different from their own. This reinforces the idea that texts are a product of the authors and illustrators who produce them, and because of this they can be "deconstructed, or questioned and critiqued" (Jones & Clark, 2007, p. 104). For Kathie, an early memory of disconnection was reading *Tales of a Fourth Grade Nothing* by Judy Blume as a child living in the suburbs, having little knowledge of life in a large New York City apartment building where one gathered with friends in Central Park instead of a backyard. While this is a benign example, for children from minoritized communities or identities, being able to articulate the disconnect between their lives and the characters, individuals, and events in the books they read can be empowering. It is not that they do not belong, it is that the authors, illustrators, and publishers may not be creating and publishing books that represent all of the diversity of our lives.

While "best of" and award lists can be a good place to begin to search for books, not all books need to be the highest quality literature for them to be included in a classroom library or even a lesson. Carter (2010), for example, makes a powerful argument that teachers can focus on "mid-level" books (p. 56) as they are the books that will engage readers and encourage them to read more. If students do not enjoy reading or listening to a book, they are less likely to associate reading with positive feelings and thus will be less likely to engage in reading for pleasure, and their reading skills will not grow as quickly as students who frequently read. However, whatever book a teacher chooses for presentation to a class, it should be the product of thoughtful analysis and consideration. In this text, we would like to argue that in addition to considering the SEL, content area, and ELA connections, a teacher should also consider the overall quality of the text, and who is represented in it.

Specific Qualities of All Types of Illustrated Texts

For any illustrated text or graphic novel, either literary or informational, there are some key characteristics to identify. For a book to be considered to be of good quality, there should be rich themes or central ideas, well-developed characters or key individuals, complex illustrations, rich language, and an engaging, multi-layered plot (Hoffman et al., 2015). These rich themes are often inferred rather than explicitly stated, encouraging readers to engage deeply with the text, and, as students progress in their reading skills, to understand that there can be multiple themes all supported by evidence in the text. The characters or key individuals in a text should be complex and dynamic, changing over the course of the book, and demonstrating the full scope of human emotions and motivations. While materials should be grade-appropriate, well-developed characters or individuals in a text are part of what makes a text valuable for SEL integration. Complex illustrations are at the heart of any picture book or graphic novel. As noted earlier, it is the interplay between visuals and text that makes for a powerful reading experience as readers use the illustrations to deepen meaning, and, at times, to consider disconnects between the text and illustrations. Unlike traditional chapter books, illustrated texts tend to have few words, either because they are traditional, shorter picture books, or because in a graphic novel the story is communicated in snippets of texts combined with pictures. These factors mean that words need to be carefully chosen. Sentences or phrases may be succinct, but still communicate an important message to upper elementary students. Finally, the plot or structure needs to engage readers. Many books for children in upper elementary grades are written about children of similar ages because this gives students an easy point of entrance to understanding the lives of others. However, because these young people are also beginning to expand their perspectives, these texts may expose students to lived experiences very different from their own, and this may spark new interests in students.

Specific Qualities of Informational Texts

While the characteristics listed above apply to both literary and informational texts, informational texts have their own set of unique characteristics. Particularly as students get older, and informational texts become denser with content-specific vocabulary, students may struggle to read these texts. There are, however, numerous factors that can support students as they read them. Weih (2015) suggests that educators begin with topics that interest their students so that students have the prior knowledge to support comprehension. Additionally, books that are creative in their presentation can draw students in, and keep them engaged with the reading experience, even if the content is difficult. Text features can also support the reader. Bold or larger text can draw readers' attention to important information, and interesting graphics can help students understand key information. While informational texts provide unique challenges for readers, the best ones draw the readers in through interesting subject matter, supportive and intriguing text features, and graphic features that help enhance comprehension.

Representation Matters

At the same time an educator is considering whether a book fits the SEL and content area or ELA objectives, and if it is a well-crafted book that will engage the students in the classroom, it is also essential to consider who is represented in the text. Our society is diverse, and students should encounter the full scope of that diversity in the world around them. The books used in the classroom should include all aspects of diversity, including race, culture, language, dis/ability, gender/sex, sexual orientation, and socioeconomic status. Strykowski (2020), for example, writes about the importance of all children finding characters they can connect to in the text they read. These experiences will allow students to "gain new ways of thinking about and relating to those who may appear different from them" (p. 52). Put another way, books should serve as both mirrors, representing the lives of the children who read them, and windows, exposing students to a world different from their own (Bishop, 1990).

Within this representation, it is also important for students to be exposed to both "average" people and heroes. Most young readers want to connect, through texts, with people who are similar to them. Teachers have to address various SEL competencies, but it can be done with diverse books that show everyday experiences (e.g., managing changes in peer groups as students mature, difficulties with parents and siblings, and trying new experiences such as sleep-away camps). In *Long Distance*, for example, a graphic novel by Whitney Gardner, the main character experiences a friendship upheaval after she moves with her family and has a unique experience at a summer camp. She also happens to have two dads. This is presented factually; it is not a plot point; it is just something that "is." For students with same-sex parents, this representation may be an invaluable validation, and for other students, this could serve as a window into the fact that some children do, in fact, have two dads (or two moms). Other books such as biographies that detail the lived experiences of heroes or people who have experienced great success can be a key component in developing the self-concept of all students but can be especially important for students in minoritized groups who may not see role models in their lives who look like them, speak like them, or have similar backgrounds. The individuals in these books can inspire and motivate students, especially when SEL-focused lessons help students understand how these individuals overcame the hardships they experienced (Abellán-Pagnani & Hébert, 2013; Floyd & Hébert, 2010).

The books chosen in an upper elementary classroom also serve the important role of acting as windows to a broader society. In many cases, students will be interacting with texts where the characters or individuals have something in common with them, perhaps they are of a similar age, or are experiencing a similar difficulty, but they might also be different in terms of race, language, etc. This allows them to both connect with the people in the text, but also learn about someone with a different set of life experiences. Whether the books are about people of color (e.g., Gatson, 2020), members of the LGBTQIA+ community (e.g., Casciola, 2013, Sciurba, 2017; Young, 2019), individuals with disabilities (e.g., Pennell, Wolak, & Koppenhaver, 2018), religious minorities, (e.g., Baer, 2017), those from lower socioeconomic groups (e.g., Quast & Bazemore-Bertrand, 2019), or individuals whose first language is not English (Koss & Daniel, 2018), research has shown the important roles that they play in the classroom. Children who identify as members of one or more of these groups experience enhanced self-esteem as they see themselves represented in books, and children who are not members of these groups see that there are similarities in their differences. While some outward components of their identities might be different, there are also places for connection through the experiences and challenges they encounter.

Given there are so many things to be taken into consideration when choosing books, two suggestions have served us well as we have familiarized ourselves with the expansive range of books for this age level. First, befriend the librarians at your local and school libraries. They can be invaluable in your search for the perfect books to use for a lesson in your classroom. Second, familiarize yourself with the numerous awards and lists created to recognize outstanding children's literature (see Table 2.1). In addition, many states have their own awards for children's books. For example, in our home state of Illinois, the Bluestem Awards (overseen by the Association of Illinois School Library Educators) allow children and educators to nominate books appealing to children in grades 3–5. The children then have the opportunity to read the books and vote on their favorite. These awards can support teaching about texts in the upper elementary grades, as students learn to analyze the texts that they enjoyed and make decisions about what makes books "quality" or not. While the books on these lists represent a variety of formats, given the popularity of illustrated books and graphic texts, you will find many examples of these types of texts, and perhaps some valuable traditional chapter books as well.

Table 2.1 Resources for Finding Quality Picture Books

Award Winners (American Library Association & Associates)

American Indian Youth Literature Award
- For writing and illustrations by and about American Indians
- https://ailanet.org/activities/american-indian-youth-literature-award

Asian/Pacific American Award
- To honor individual work about Asian/Pacific Americans and their heritage
- https://www.apalaweb.org/awards/literature-awards

Pura Belpré Award
- For a Latino/Latina writer and illustrator whose work best portrays, affirms, and celebrates the Latino cultural experience
- https://www.ala.org/alsc/awardsgrants/bookmedia/belpre

Randolph Caldecott Medal
- For the most distinguished American picture book for children
- https://www.ala.org/alsc/awardsgrants/bookmedia/caldecott

Coretta Scott King Award
- For outstanding African American authors and illustrators of books that demonstrate an appreciation of African American culture and universal human values
- https://www.ala.org/rt/emiert/cskbookawards

John Newbery Medal
- For the most distinguished contribution to American literature for children
- https://www.ala.org/alsc/awardsgrants/bookmedia/newbery

Rainbow Book List
- An annual annotated bibliography consisting of quality LGBTQIA+ literature
- https://www.ala.org/awardsgrants/rainbow-project-book-list

Rise: A Feminist Book Project
- An annotated book list focused on books with significant feminist content
- https://risefeministbooks.wordpress.com/book-lists

Schneider Family Book Award
- Presented to an author or illustrator for a book that embodies an artistic expression of the disability experience
- www.ala.org/awardsgrants/schneider-family-book-award

Robert F. Sibert Informational Book Medal
- For the most distinguished informational book published in the United States in English
- https://www.ala.org/alsc/awardsgrants/bookmedia/sibert

Stonewall Book Awards
- For English language books that have exceptional merit relating to the LGBTQIA+ experience
- https://www.ala.org/rt/rrt/award/stonewall/honored

Sydney Taylor Book Award
- For books that authentically portray the Jewish experience
- https://jewishlibraries.org/sydney_taylor_book_award

Choosing Quality Books ◆ 35

Journals, Magazines, and Newspapers with Online Reviews

The Horn Book
www.hbook.com

Booklist
www.booklistonline.com

School Library Journal
www.slj.com

Kirkus Reviews
www.kirkusreviews.com

Publishers Weekly
www.publishersweekly.com

The New York Times
www.nytimes.com/column/childrens-books

Web Resources

Social Justice Book Lists
- More than 80 carefully selected lists of multicultural and social justice books
- https://socialjusticebooks.org/booklists

Goodreads
- A site that creates lists based on readers' reviews
- www.goodreads.com

Children's Literature Portraying Religious Diversity in the US
- Lists of quality books that focus on authentic expressions of religious diversity for children grades K–4
- https://lib.stpetersburg.usf.edu/ChildrensLiteratureReligiousDiversity/MultipleReligions

We Need Diverse Books
- Advocacy organization that promotes changes in the publishing industry to promote and produce diverse children's literature
- Presents the Walter Award for diverse authors of books for ages 9–13 and teens
- www.diversebooks.org

Other Resources

Bank Street Best Children's Books of the Year
- Annual publication by the Children's Book Committee that aims to guide educators, librarians, and caregivers to the best children's books published each year
- https://www.bankstreet.edu/library/center-for-childrens-literature/childrens-book-committee/best-childrens-books-of-the-year

Orbis Pictus Award
- Awarded by the National Council of Teachers of English for excellence in the writing of nonfiction for children
- https://ncte.org/awards/orbis-pictus-award-non-fiction-for-children

Connecting Books to SEL

Instead of thinking of SEL as one additional area to teach, it is helpful to view SEL integration as an extension of content and literacy learning. While the criteria are different depending on whether you are searching for books to integrate STEM, social studies, or ELA into your lessons, you can view each through an SEL lens. The CASEL competencies (i.e., self-awareness, self-management, social awareness, relationship skills, and responsible decision-making) will be found in many of the books that you have chosen for your lessons, making integration almost seamless. From an SEL perspective, this integration can also be powerful because rather than having a stand-alone SEL time, students can consider these topics and competencies while they discuss the behaviors of characters and individuals in a book. For some children, this may also provide a level of safety. Rather than discussing their own struggles, they can reflect on the difficulties of the people in the texts, and identify ways they can apply their learning to their own lives.

Additionally, a review of the Common Core State Standards and other national standards documents provides support for the goal of integrating SEL with learning in ELA and the content areas. For example, the Common Core Standards document points out that students who have met the standards will "come to understand other perspectives and cultures" (NGACBP & CCSSO, 2010, p. 7). This clear connection shows that as students interact with texts through reading, writing, and listening and speaking, they will be exposed to ideas and experiences that are different from their own lives. Specifically, looking at the CASEL competencies, there is a connection to social awareness and relationship skills, but it is not difficult to see that developing an understanding of others can also support self-awareness and self-management, particularly when one is tempted to judge another person based on one's own personal perspective. Additionally, in the C3 Social Studies framework document, the introductory materials note that students must be "aware of their changing cultural and physical environments" and "act in ways that promote the common good" (NCSS, 2013, p. 5). As with the

Common Core, it is clear that the cognitive, social, and emotional components of SEL can be addressed in unison with the content area standards.

A word of warning, in choosing books, teachers must be aware of the lived experiences of their students. While it is important to expose children to the experiences of others, educators should be alert to situations where in the process of increasing empathy and compassion in one group of children, often those from majority cultures, other children are made to feel uncomfortable or are perhaps traumatized (Katch, 2018). If this were to be a concern, a conversation with the parents, or, if appropriate, the children themselves might help a teacher decide whether or not to move forward with a particular text. Additionally, sometimes, texts can stir up difficult feelings and memories, and children should be reassured that they have ownership over their life stories. No child should ever feel pressured to share experiences if that might be difficult for them. Students can also be reminded that they, and their peers, only speak for themselves. No one is responsible for speaking for or representing an entire group of people.

Diverse graphic texts can be instructional for both students and teachers. Teachers, whatever their sets of life experiences, cannot possibly be aware of all of the backgrounds of their students. By researching diverse books and authors, they may find themselves expanding their knowledge of the cultural capital of the children in their classrooms. As children get older, they may also be willing to share recommendations for books to include in a classroom library or lessons. This knowledge can then be transformed into more fully informed "culturally relevant" teaching practices. It is well established that when students have a healthy self-concept and pride in their cultural identity, their academic success will increase. Gloria Ladson-Bilings (1995), who introduced the term "culturally relevant pedagogy," noted, "Culturally relevant teachers utilize students' culture as a vehicle for learning" (p. 161) and provided several examples from her research of the positive effect this had on students' academic success. By making thoughtful book choices, teachers can increase their knowledge and have a positive influence on both the students' self-concept and their academic achievement.

In popular culture, the term "unicorn" is used to refer to something rare or highly valued. While perhaps not as rare as an actual unicorn, finding the perfect book in a classroom can, at times, feel a bit like the search for a unicorn. To begin with, a teacher can only share a finite number of books with students in a given year, so decisions must be made thoughtfully. Is the book well written and illustrated? Will the book engage the students? Does it provide a representation of differences both in the book and who is writing it? Does it teach the content and/or literacy skills needed? Does it match the SEL competency? And, as we think about growing future readers, particularly at a time when students may be less likely to choose to read, does the book encourage students to read other books in the series, by the author, or on the same topic or theme? Does it help us grow future readers? While the search may be challenging, the feeling of sharing the "perfect" book with a student or class is worth the work.

References

Abellán-Pagnani, L. & Hébert, T. P. (2013). Using picture books to guide and inspire young gifted Hispanic students. *Gifted Child Today*, (*36*)1: 47–56. DOI: 10.1177/1076217512459735

American Library Association (ALA). (2023, February 26). *Randolph Caldecott Medal*. American Library Association. https://www.ala.org/alsc/awardsgrants/bookmedia/caldecott

American Library Association (ALA) Graphic Novels and Comics Round Table. (2023, February 26). *Best graphic novels – FAQ*. ALA. https://www.ala.org/rt/gncrt/-bgna-faq

Baer, A. L. (2017). Beyond the veil: Exploring Muslim cultures through children's picture books. *Ohio Journal of English Language Arts*, (*57*)1: 23–29.

Bishop R. S. (1990). Mirrors, windows, and sliding glass doors. *Perspectives*, *6*(3): ix–xi.

Carter, B. (2010, July/August). Not the Newbury: Books that make the reader. *The Horn Book Magazine*, *86*(4): 52–56.

Casciola, V. (2013). Creating a space for all children: Providing LGBTQ literature in the classroom. *Journal of Reading Education*, *39*(1): 34–35.

Floyd, E. F. & Hébert, T. P. (2010). Using picture book biographies. *Gifted Child Today*, *33*(2): 38–46.

Harvey, S. & Goudvis, A. (2017). *Strategies that work: Teaching comprehension to enhance understanding* (3rd ed.). Stenhouse.

Hoffman J. L., Teale, W. H., & Yokota, J. (2015). The book matters! Choosing complex narrative texts to support literacy discussions. *Young Children, 70*(4): 8–15.

Jones, S. & Clarke, L. W. (2007). Disconnections: Pushing readers beyond connections and toward the critical. *Pedagogies: An International Journal, 2*(2): 95–115. DOI: 10.1080/15544800701484069

Katch, J. (2018). Seeing me in you: Teaching empathy and learning courage through picture books. *Schools: Studies in Education, 15*(2): 216–227.

Keene, E. & Zimmerman, S. (2007). *Mosaic of thought: The power of comprehension strategy instruction* (2nd ed.). Heinemann.

Koss, M. D. and Daniel, M. C. (2018). Valuing the lives and experiences of English learners: Widening the landscape of children's literature. *TESOL Journal, 9*(4): 431–454. DOI: 10.1002/tesj.336

Ladson-Bilings, G. (1995). But that's just good teaching! The case for culturally relevant pedagogy. *Theory into Practice, 34*(3): 159–165.

McClanahan, M. & Nottingham, M. (2019). A suite of strategies for navigating graphic novels: A dual coding approach. *The Reading Teacher, 73*(1): 39–50.

National Council for the Social Studies (NCSS). (2013). *The College, Career, and Civic Life (C3) Framework for Social Studies State Standards: Guidance for enhancing the rigor of K-12 civics, economics, geography, and history.* NCSS.

National Governors Association Center for Best Practices and Council of Chief State School (NGACBP & CCSSO) (2010). *Common Core State Standards: English language arts and literacy in history/social studies, science, and technical subjects.* Authors. http://www.corestandards.org/wp-content/uploads/ELA_Standards.pdf

Pennell, A. E., Wollak, B., & Koppenhaver, D. A. (2018). Respectful representations of disability in picture books. *The Reading Teacher, 71*(4): 411–419.

Quast, E. & Bazemore-Bertrand, S. (2019). Exploring economic diversity and inequity through picture books. *The Reading Teacher, 73*(2): 219–222. DOI:10.1002/trtr.1807

Rodriguez, S. C., Gonzalez, K., & Rojas, C. (2020). Immigration picture books by #ownvoices authors. *Georgia Journal of Literacy, 43*(2): Article 5. Retrieved February 15, 2021, from https://digitalcommons.kennesaw.edu/gjl/vol43/iss2/5

Sciurba, K. (2017). Flowers, dancing, dresses, and dolls: Picture book representations of gender-variant males. *Children's Literature in Education*, *48*(3): 276–293.

Serafini, F. (2011). Creating space for children's literature. *The Reading Teacher*, *65*(1): 30–34. DOI:10.1598/RT.65.1.4

Serafini, F. (2014). *Reading the visual: An introduction to teaching multimodal literacy*. Teachers College Press.

Sipe, L. R. (1998). How children's books work: A semiotically framed theory of text-picture relationships. *Children's Literature in Education*, *29*(2): 97–108.

Smith, J. M. & Pole, K. (2018). What's going on in a graphic novel? *The Reading Teacher*, *72*(2): 169–177.

Strykowski, M. (2020). Choosing books for today's children. *Knowledge Quest*, *48*(4): 50–52.

Weih, T. G. (2015). *How to select books for teaching to children: Taking a critical look at books through a pedagogical lens*. University of Northern Iowa. https://files.eric.ed.gov/fulltext/ED554313.pdf

Wolfenberger, C. D. & Sipe, L. R. (2007). A unique visual and literary art form: Recent research on picture books. *Language Arts*, *84*(3): 273–280.

Young, C. A. (2019). Interrogating the lack of diversity in award-winning LGBTQ-inclusive picturebooks. *Theory Into Practice*, *58*(1): 61–70.

Book List

Blume, J. (2007). *Tales of a fourth grade nothing*. Puffin Books. (Original work published 1972.)

Castrovilla, S. (2022). *Seeking freedom: The untold story of Fortress Monroe and the ending of slavery in America* (E. B. Lewis, Illus.). Calkins Creek.

Frazee, M. (2008). *A couple of boys have the best week ever* (M. Frazee, Illus.). Clarion Books.

Gardiner, J. R. (2010). *Stone Fox* (G. Hargreaves, Illus.). Harper Collins. (Original work published 1980.)

Gardner, W. (2021). *Long distance* (W. Gardner, Illus.). Simon & Schuster Books Young Readers.

Klaussen, J. (2011). *I want my hat back* (J. Klaussen, Illus.). Candlewick.

3

Matching Children to Books

Chapter 2 focused on identifying quality illustrated texts and graphic novels that teachers could use to support the integration of SEL into teaching in the content areas and ELA. The metaphor used was that finding the perfect book that was high quality, representative of the diversity in the classroom and broader world, and addressed the SEL competencies and the content or ELA content, skills, and strategies was much like looking for a unicorn. This chapter adds yet another layer of complexity: the importance of matching children to books that meet their interests, maturity level, and academic needs. As you begin to identify which books will be a good fit for the children in your classroom, you can begin to ask questions such as: What content and/or standards does this book need to support? What are the reading strengths and challenges of the students who will read or listen to the book? What tasks will they complete based on the book? What are their interests? What are their identities? What is the maturity level of the students?

While there are some disagreements among researchers, overall, experts in the field of literacy agree that for children to grow as readers, they need to read books that provide a significant amount of independent fluent reading, but also small challenges in vocabulary, text structures, and genre that encourage students to develop their skills as readers (Allington et al., 2015). It is also important to note that researchers distinguish between *text complexity* and *text difficulty*. *Text complexity* refers to the characteristics of the text without considering the readers, whereas *text difficulty* considers the interaction between reader and text (Amendum et al., 2018, Sierschynsk et al., 2014). This means that the measure of text complexity will not change from reader to reader. The words will still have the same number of syllables, sentences will be the same length, etc. Text difficulty, however, does change based on the characteristics of the reader. A book that may seem difficult to one student may seem easy in the hands of another student who has a lot of background information on the topic, or extensive experience with a genre or author.

This chapter builds on the characteristics of quality texts delineated in Chapter 2. A quality text should be expertly crafted, including well-developed characters or individuals, and carefully created visuals, as well as authors and characters that represent the diversity of the world around us. Additionally, teachers must also consider the unique characteristics of their students, and how books may or may not match the child's needs. You will likely find as you read this chapter that matching children to books is as much an "art" as it is a "science." While a book may be appropriate based on the qualitative and quantitative measures described here, it may not draw a child in. Our university students often ask as they begin a lesson plan assignment or try to decide on a book to bring to their clinical experiences if a particular book is "right" or "appropriate" for a group of students. Unfortunately, our answers are usually a very unsatisfying version of "it depends." Matching children to books depends on so many things, and this chapter attempts to provide a starting place for deliberations as it delineates three areas of text complexity to consider: quantitative measures, qualitative measures, and reader and task factors.

Quantitative Measures

While any system of identifying a "best fit" book for a child has its limitations, for many educators, the initial process of matching children and texts begins with an assessment of a student's reading level and a quantitative measure of text complexity.

Many states' standardized test score reports come with a Lexile level for each student, but there are other planned assessment processes (e.g., Guided Reading, Accelerated Reader) that result in a level being assigned to the students to indicate their reading ability. Using online tools such as Scholastic's "Book Wizard" or Lexile's "Find a Book," an educator can enter a book title and be given a level or find books within a given reading level range. The Lexile website also has an additional tool that allows an educator to upload a portion of text for analysis and leveling. Despite the relative ease of matching a student to a book using a quantitative measure, this should only be one of several considerations, and the following description of how quantitative measures work will illustrate why relying solely on these measures can be problematic when attempting to find the best books for students.

Lexile measures are a commonly used scale for determining a text's complexity, although there are others. This quantitative scale uses word frequency and sentence length to determine a level for a text. Students are also assigned a Lexile level based on their reading abilities. The Lexile Framework then suggests that students read texts that are from 100 below their current level to 50 above. For example, a fourth-grade student who is evaluated to be reading at a 740 Lexile level would be encouraged to read texts between 640L and 790L. However, even within this set of quantitative measures of text complexity and student reading ability, there are indicators that demonstrate that this framework does not encompass all of the unique characteristics of children's literature.

The Lexile system also includes a set of codes that provides additional information about texts that help as educators and parents endeavor to guide children toward appropriate books. In addition to the codes like GN for "graphic novel" and "IG" for "illustrated guide" (for non-fiction reference books) that provide information about the format of the text, there are also codes that provide information about the content of the text and for which readers, or in which context, the book might be best used. AD, for example, means "adult-directed," NC means "non-conforming," and "HL" means high-low. An "adult-directed" book would be best read aloud by an adult because of complexities in the topic, text difficulty, or book layout. An example of an adult-directed book using the Lexile Framework is *Malala, a Brave Girl from Pakistan/Iqbal, a Brave Boy from Pakistan* by Jeannette Winter. While the Lexile level of 640L places it at a second-grade level, the issue of child slavery, the denial of girls' rights to education, and the violence against both children make it a book that children should be guided through, not one given to a child to read independently. The GN code is important to consider, particularly given the interplay between words and visuals described in Chapter 2. While many graphic novels will have lower Lexile levels, because of the limited text and shorter vocabulary, given the complexities of "reading" both the text and visuals to make meaning of the story, they may not be appropriate for all younger readers. Additionally, the topics and themes in graphic novels intended for children in upper elementary school may not be appropriate for younger children.

The codes NC (non-conforming) and "HL" (high-low) can also help educators who are trying to find books on a common topic or theme that meet the needs of a variety of learners in their classroom, from students reading significantly below grade level to students reading significantly above. The code NC will indicate a book that has a higher reading level but is still age-appropriate. For example, books in the Series of Unfortunate Events series by Lemony Snicket, including *The Penultimate Peril* and *The End* are given the NC code. These books are at more challenging reading levels but are still appropriate for younger readers who have the skills to handle them. HL books, conversely, are listed as such because they are highly engaging for older children, but at a lower reading level. *Take the Plunge*, the second book in The InvestiGators series by John Green is a good example. It has a lower Lexile level (410L) but has content of interest to upper elementary and middle school students. These readers may struggle to read books written at grade level, but books with an HL distinction generally include content that would engage older readers.

Qualitative Measures

While it may seem like an extra step to go beyond the quantitative measures, especially given the extra detail the Lexile

Framework provides, it is important to understand that using a quantitative measure to match students to books should only be seen as a first step. Qualitative measures, those that require the judgment of an informed reader, are a powerful component of matching children to books for two key reasons. First, these measures provide a level of nuance and judgment that is not available with a quantitative measure. Second, the process of analyzing a text to understand its complexity provides educators with insights into the book that can be helpful beyond the task of matching books to readers. The knowledge gained can be used to create lesson plans that address the necessary ELA skills and strategies for the grade level. Additionally, as noted before, there are a number of instances when a quantitative measure might lead you astray. A book can have fairly simple sentences and words but have themes or topics that are not appropriate for the students, or a book can have a fairly simple topic or theme, but be written in such a way, for example with figurative language, multiple changes in perspective, or complex vocabulary, that the book is not appropriate for younger or less proficient readers.

There are four main areas for consideration within the broader concept of qualitative measures. These are: levels of meaning or purpose, structure, language conventionality and clarity, and knowledge demands. Table 3.1 suggests questions that can guide reviewers as they consider the complexity of the text. While there are some differences between informational and literary texts, the key ideas are similar regardless of the text type.

While the considerations in Table 3.1 are applicable to all text formats, when considering graphic novels or picture books that may include some characteristics of graphic novels, it is particularly important to consider the "structure" questions. For example, a graphic novel might include dialogue presented in a variety of different ways. Colors, capitals vs. lower-case letters, size, font, etc. might all change to convey different meanings. Readers who are not familiar with these methods of conveying meaning, or have not been taught to consider them explicitly, might miss out on important aspects of the plot. Similarly, with regard to the illustrations in a graphic novel, it is not uncommon

Table 3.1 Questions for Considering Text Complexity Using Qualitative Factors

Qualitative Factor	Questions to Ask
Levels of Meaning or Purpose	• Is there one level of meaning, or are there multiple levels of meaning? (literary text) • Is the purpose explicitly stated, or must it be inferred? (informational text)
Structure	• Is the organization simple or complex, and are connections explicit or implicit? • Is the structure conventional or unconventional? • Are events presented chronologically/logically, or are there jumps in time or flashbacks? • Are the traits common to a genre or a unique disciplinary structure? (especially informational text) • Are the graphics simple or complex? • Are the graphics relevant and supportive of the readers' meaning-making?
Language Conventionality and Clarity	• Is the language primarily literal or figurative/ironic? • Is the language clear or ambiguous/purposefully misleading? • Is the language contemporary or familiar, or archaic or otherwise unfamiliar? • Is the language conversational, or does the text contain numerous general academic or domain-specific words?
Knowledge Demands: Life Experiences (literary texts)	• Is the theme simple or complex/sophisticated? • Is there a single theme, or are there multiple themes? • Are the experiences common, everyday experiences or clearly fantastical situations? Are the experiences distinctly different from the reader's own? • Is there a single perspective or multiple perspectives? • Are the perspective(s) similar to the reader's, or are they unlike or in opposition to the reader's perspective?
Knowledge Demands: Cultural/Literary Knowledge (chiefly literary texts)	• Does comprehension require everyday knowledge and familiarity with common genre conventions, or is additional cultural and literary knowledge useful? • Are there few references or allusions to other texts (low intertextuality), or are there many references/allusions (high intertextuality)?
Knowledge Demands: Content/Discipline Knowledge (chiefly informational texts)	• Does comprehension require everyday knowledge and familiarity with common genre conventions, or is extensive content knowledge required? • Are there few references to/citations of other texts (low intertextuality), or are there many references to/citations of other texts (high intertextuality)?

Source: Adapted from: *Common Core State Standards for English language arts and literacy in history/social studies, science, and technical subjects: Appendix A: Research supporting key elements of the standards and glossary of key terms.*

for an illustrator to demonstrate the passage of time from day to evening not in words, but through the color of the sky in panels. If this change is not obvious, a reader's understanding of the text could be negatively impacted.

Reader and Task Factors

Although the qualitative and quantitative considerations related to text complexity are not simple, they are perhaps more easily considered than the reader and task factors discussed in this section. Quantitative factors have their limitations, but once the Lexile number is assigned, it is consistent. Qualitative factors rely on the expert judgment of the reader, but it is not hard to imagine a group of teachers reading and reviewing the books that they plan to use in their classrooms in the upcoming year, discussing and coming to a consensus on the qualitative levels of complexity, based on the questions noted in the previous section. These two factors are based on the text, whereas reader and task factors are external to the text. While potentially challenging to identify, they are an essential component of matching children to books.

While many teachers might begin with a quantitative measure of text complexity, and then adjust the book up or down depending on their review of qualitative factors, some researchers argue that reader and task factors should be considered first. For example, Wixson and Valencia (2014) state: "We suggest that reader and task factors be among the first considerations in measuring text complexity because they are likely to be the most important factors in determining the comprehension of complex text in a specific instructional context" (p. 431). They remind educators that the complex process of matching children to books must consider text, reader, and task together.

When considering reader factors, the RAND Reading Study Group (2002) noted three categories of factors that impact students' abilities to read: cognitive capacities, motivation, and knowledge, and experiences. Thinking about children you have taught or encountered in your life, you can likely identify students who, "on paper" were not the strongest readers, but with a combination of motivation or life experiences were able to successfully comprehend books that were beyond their identified reading level. Conversely, you may have also encountered students who, despite strong reading scores, struggled with a text that did not interest them or for which they did not have significant background knowledge. The work of the RAND group reminds all educators that while cognitive abilities and knowledge of vocabulary and topic are important, equally important are the students' sense of self-efficacy, their interest in the text, and their understanding of the purpose for reading. In the upper elementary grades, students may be motivated to read what their peers are reading or be able to read a more complex text related to an area of interest. It is not uncommon at this age for children to begin to venture, for example, into the adult non-fiction section of the public library to find books to support their learning about a hobby or to provide more in-depth information on a topic of great interest. For this reason, reader factors are a key area to consider when matching children to books.

In addition, there are three task factors to consider. These are: the level of support students will be given as they read, the complexity of the task they are being asked to complete as a result of the reading, and the intended consequence of the reading. First, when considering support, students will be able to manage a more complex text if there is scaffolded support through a read-aloud, a guided reading group, or even frequent opportunities for confirming understanding through small group or whole class discussions. The greater the teacher's role in facilitation, the more able students will be to manage a complex text (Valencia et al., 2014). These instructional activities allow teachers to assess students' understanding informally, provide clarification about key information or plot points, define essential vocabulary, etc. Additionally, as noted previously, there are also texts that might be best used in an "adult-directed" setting because they contain more mature topics and themes. Furthermore, the typical instructional choices that a teacher might make such as a quick write, a turn and talk, or posing questions at different levels of comprehension will all provide insight into students' understanding, and the teacher will be able to adjust instruction accordingly. This support allows a more challenging text to be made appropriate for students.

Second, the task students are asked to complete as a result of the reading also plays a major role in whether or not a student can handle a complex text. For example, asking students to identify main characters and plot points is a more concrete task than asking students to find themes or compare and contrast the actions of two characters. As part of the decision-making process, as students are matched to texts, it will be important to consider what students will be expected to do. Wixson and Valencia (2014) note that altering a learning task can "change the difficulty of the text and students' ability to deeply comprehend" (p. 432). In other words, a simpler task can make a challenging text seem easier, a more complex task can make an easier text seem more challenging.

Finally, as readers, we all engage with texts for different purposes. If you think through the types of reading you have done in a day or a week, odds are, your reading experiences will fall into one of three categories: Knowledge, application, or engagement (RAND, 2002). As a teacher, you might read an article to find out about an author whose books you are about to share with your class (knowledge), you might read the instruction manual to make the best use of the newest piece of education technology in your classroom (application), or you might read a book "for fun" for the book club you and some of your colleagues attend (engagement). For upper elementary readers, whose opinions about reading may already be somewhat solidified, finding books that have a purpose for the students beyond "doing school" can be particularly valuable. These students may be better able to manage more challenging texts when they see a purpose in their lives for the knowledge or application, or engage with the book because they are interested in it, or because it connects them with their peers.

Thinking about reader and task factors also provides teachers with an ideal opportunity for differentiation. Perhaps one text is expected to be read by all students in a particular classroom or grade level. The text would be appropriate for some readers, too challenging for others, and too simple for yet another group of students. However, if teachers can consider how to increase or decrease the amount of support they give students, provide a variety of tasks at differing levels of complexity, and/or change the intended consequence of the reading, more students will be able to interact appropriately with the common text.

Unique Needs of Upper Elementary Students

By the upper elementary years, many students may have already identified themselves as "good readers" or "bad readers," or may quickly explain to anyone who will listen that they either "love" or "hate" reading. As teachers ponder how to choose texts for their class, and consider what books to suggest to specific students, there are some tips that can help. At this age, particularly for struggling readers, setting students up for success with texts they can read fluently is particularly important, and children are more likely to want to read if the topic interests them or is something a friend is reading. Books in a series can help here, because if a student has read one book in a series that they enjoyed, subsequent books in the series will have similar structures, content, and vocabulary. Finally, graphic novels can also make readers feel more accomplished because, while they have a limited number of words, they are the same length as many chapter books, so readers can move through them relatively quickly while still reading a lengthy text (Swaggerty, 2015).

For readers of all abilities, there should be numerous opportunities to read texts that both reinforce existing reading skills as well as allow for self-teaching as students work through complex concepts in books at an appropriate level of challenge. In this sense, the text diet mentioned in Chapter 2 also applies to the challenge level of books children are reading. Mesmer, Cunningham, and Hiebert (2012), for example, note that a readers' diet of text "provides and limits their opportunities to benefit from points of overlap between text complexity and reading instruction" (p. 247). When books are a good fit for readers, they are both solidifying the skills and strategies students have already learned and also providing new challenges where students can use what they have previously learned in new reading situations, as well as learn new skills and strategies. For this reason, the process of matching children to books is like trying to reach a goalpost that keeps moving. The RAND Reading Study Group (2002), for example, states: "As a reader begins to read and completes whatever activity is at hand, some of the knowledge and capabilities of the reader change" (p. 13). The child is learning and growing with each text, whilst while they are reading. However, an educator who is knowledgeable about the interplay of quantitative, qualitative, and reader and task factors in understanding text complexity will also be more adept at matching children to books, identifying mismatches, and suggesting changes to a reader's text diet when necessary.

References

Allington, R. L., McCuiston, K., & Billen, M. (2015). What research says about text complexity and learning to read. *Reading Teacher, 68*(7): 491–501.

Amendum, S. J., Conradi, K., & Hieber, E. (2018). Does text complexity matter in the elementary grades? A research synthesis of text difficulty and elementary students' reading fluency and comprehension. *Educational Psychology Review, 30*(1): 121–151.

Mesmer, H. A., Cunningham, J. W., & Hiebert, E. H. (2012). Toward a theoretical model of text complexity for the early grades: Learning from the past, anticipating the future. *Reading Research Quarterly, 47*: 235–258. DOI:10.1002/rrq.019

MetaMetrics. (2024, March 15). *Understanding Lexile® measures.* https://lexile.com/educators/understanding-lexile-measures

RAND Reading Study Group. (2002). *Reading for understanding: Toward an R&D program in reading comprehension.* RAND.

Sierschynsk, J., Louie, B., & Pughe, B. (2014). Complexity in picture books. *Reading Teacher, 68*(4): 287–295.

Swaggerty, E. A. (2015). Selecting engaging texts for upper elementary students who avoid reading or find reading difficult. In D. A. Wooten & B. E. Cullinan (Eds.), *Children's literature in the reading program: Engaging young readers in the 21st century* (4th ed., pp. 150–166). International Literacy Association.

Valencia, S. W., Wixson, K. K., & Pearson, P. D. (2014). Putting text complexity in context: Refocusing on comprehension of complex text. *The Elementary School Journal, 115*(2): 270–289. DOI:10.1086/678296

Wixson, K. K. & S. W. Valencia. (2014). CCSS-ELA suggestions and cautions for addressing text complexity. *Reading Teacher, 67*(6): 430–434.

Book List

Green, J. P. (2020). *InvestiGators: Take the plunge* (J. Green, Illus.). Macmillan Children's Books.

Snicket, L. (2005). *A series of unfortunate events: The penultimate peril*. HarperCollins.

Snicket, L. (2006). *A series of unfortunate events: The end*. HarperCollins.

Winter, J. (2014). *Malala, a brave girl from Pakistan/Iqbal, a brave boy from Pakistan* (1st ed.). Beach Lane Books.

4

Integrating SEL and Subject Content in Lesson Plans

The core components of SEL are already fundamental components of general K-12 curricula, and consequently it is a straightforward step to incorporate SEL competencies and domains into the specific content areas of social studies, Science, Technology, Engineering, and Mathematics (STEM), and ELA. This chapter will examine how SEL domains and competencies can be integrated throughout the grades 3–5 curricula of social studies, STEM, and ELA, as well as in cross-curricular lessons with multiple subjects. In all three subjects, the SEL themes can be taught both through the subject content and in the exercises and activities of the lesson. The first section of this chapter will give an overview of the SEL competencies of CASEL as they relate to the core subjects of social studies, STEM, and ELA. It will provide examples of how to incorporate SEL themes in the specific subjects using graphic texts, with differentiation techniques for classrooms. The chapter will conclude with an example of how to build a lesson plan that incorporates the subject content, SEL domains, and an accompanying book.

Teaching SEL Through Subject Content

Social and emotional themes appear in the content and the curricula and pedagogy of key subject content, including social

DOI: 10.4324/9781003406662-5

studies, ELA, and STEM. Key social and emotional learning domains and themes are present throughout the content of the core courses, providing a multitude of examples for students to examine and discuss. For example, descriptions of historical, political, and social events provide examples of the CASEL competencies of responsible decision-making, problem-solving, and communication. Biographies of political leaders, educators, explorers, inventors, artists, and other historically important figures can be tied to such SEL competencies as self-management—setting personal and collective goals or using planning and organizational skills—and responsible decision-making. Stories of justice and unfairness provide examples of the CASEL domain of social awareness, which calls for "identifying diverse social norms, including unjust ones . . . recognizing situational demands and opportunities, [and] understanding the influences of organizations and systems on behavior" (CASEL, 2020). Real-life examples of creativity, determination, and persistence provide rich opportunities for SEL lessons around nurturing optimism, courage, gratitude, and hope and developing a growth mindset, grit, and perseverance.

Teaching SEL Through Pedagogy, Activities, and Exercises

Social and emotional themes can also be demonstrated through the subjects' pedagogy, activities, and exercises, particularly in hands-on subjects such as STEM and art. As students develop a mastery of the subject content details, they can work on projects that help them develop such SEL skills as fostering good communication, working through conflicts, overcoming failure, and practicing troubleshooting and problem-solving techniques. In class discussions and through peer reviews, students learn to respectfully share their opinions on other students' work and accept others' feedback on their own work, a skill that is included in several of the Common Core standards. Class-wide, small group, and individual activities and projects help students develop their executive functioning skills, such as project planning, task initiation, and maintaining attention and focus. Management of conflicts, a skill that is needed from the earliest ages, is a vital SEL skill that students can work on through projects with any size group, in all core subjects.

The Role of Illustrated Texts

The social and emotional skills that are demonstrated and taught through the text and illustrations of illustrated texts touch all areas of a child's life, from their emotions and interactions with others to their perspective, social- and self-awareness, and their sense of identity and responsibilities in the world. Through the actions of their characters, picture books demonstrate cognitive skills, such as executive functioning skills, problem-solving, task initiation, and time management. Graphic novels and illustrated texts are an excellent tool to bridge the subject's content and pedagogy with SEL domains through the books' plots, characters, dialogue, and images. A wide variety of fiction and non-fiction genres including historical fiction, biographies and autobiographies, poetry, mixed-media works, and graphic novels offer different perspectives and methods of approaching the text. Varying levels of complexity in the text, content matter, and visual presentation provide opportunities for differentiation within lessons for all levels of students. The difficulty levels of the books vary based on the reading level and amount of text, the use of illustrations and images, and the subject matter.

SEL Domains

Table 4.1 lists the five CASEL domains and examples of questions related to each. For example, questions that help students think about the SEL domain of self-awareness focus on having students identify the emotions that the characters in the book felt and discuss how the characters acted on those emotions. Students can

Table 4.1 CASEL domains and example questions

SEL Domain	Example Questions
Self-awareness	How did the emotions and actions of the character/person influence their behavior? Did they show biases or prejudices? Did they show a growth mindset and sense of purpose?
Self-management	How did the characters/people make plans and act on them? How did they show self-discipline and self-motivation? How did they manage their stress and emotions?
Social awareness	Did the people/characters show an understanding of other people's perspectives, emotions, and feelings? Did they share their gratitude? Did they realize how other people and organizations have an impact on the world?
Relationship skills	How did the character/person work with other people? Did they offer support, or stand up for other people? Did they have positive relationships with other people? How did they manage conflicts?
Responsible decision-making	Did the characters/people make good decisions, evaluating the problem and using good judgment to decide how to respond? Did they think about the impact of their decisions on other people and situations?

Source: *CASEL'S SEL Framework: What are the core competence areas and where are they promoted?* (2020). CASEL. www.casel.org/what-is-SEL

then consider the biases or prejudices that are presented through the characters' words and actions.

The questions related to each SEL domain can be used to tailor the subject content to the SEL themes. The next section will give examples of how SEL themes can be woven into subject lessons in each of the three core subjects of LA, social studies, and STEM, through both the subject content and the exercises with the use of illustrated texts.

Social Studies

One of the strongest subject areas for incorporating SEL themes in content curricula is social studies. Designed by the National

Council for the Social Studies to enhance social studies instruction in K-12 schools, *The College, Career, and Civic Life (C3) Framework for Social Studies State Standards* calls for students to be prepared for college, career, and civil life:

> Advocates of citizenship education cross the political spectrum, but they are bound by a common belief that our democratic republic will not sustain unless students are aware of their changing cultural and physical environments; know the past; read, write, and think deeply; and act in ways that promote the common good. There will always be differing perspectives on these objectives. The goal of knowledgeable, thinking, and active citizens, however, is universal.
> (National Council for the Social Studies, 2013)

Illustrated texts that address topics within social studies offer powerful examples of SEL themes that are demonstrated through the actions and interactions of people, in historical events, and in the creation and collapse of political, social, and economic institutions. Students can make connections with the characters and events by seeing their own history reflected in the stories, or they can expand their understanding of others' lives and challenges by learning about new life experiences that are different from their own. Graphic texts show people in the roles of heroes and ordinary people, as problem-solvers and advocates, and as flawed, persistent, learning, failing, and growing. The interplay of the books' images and text support a multitude of opportunities to learn about the events and characters while building critical-thinking skills and integrating SEL concepts such as developing relationship skills and responsible decision-making.

A National Book Award finalist that weaves SEL themes into the social studies theme of identity and community is *When Stars Are Scattered*, a graphic novel about Somali brothers growing up in a Kenyan refugee camp, as told by Omar Mohamed, a Somali refugee, to the author/illustrator, Victoria Jamieson, and colorist Iman Geddy. The book makes links with numerous SEL competencies and domains and provides powerful questions to examine:

- **Self-awareness:** How did Omar show a sense of purpose and determination in adapting to the new living situation of the Dadaab refugee camp?
- **Self-management:** How did Omar set goals for himself and use planning and organizational skills to build a new life for himself and his brother?
- **Relationship skills:** What were some examples of Omar showing strong relationship skills, such as effective communication, problem-solving, showing leadership, and standing up for the rights of others?
- **Responsible decision-making:** Were any of Omar's decisions and actions examples of using his role to work for the well-being of himself and his brother? How did his decisions and actions fit in with the community?

A non-fiction social studies topic that is powerfully presented in illustrated texts is immigration and the adaptation and adjustments of immigrants to their new home. Examples include *Isla to Island* by Alexis Castellanos, which tells the story of a Cuban girl, Marisol, who is sent from her home in Cuba to New York in the 1960s, and *Pashmina* by Nidhi Chanani, in which a girl, Priyanka, tries to understand why her mother left her father and homeland, India, to come to the United States. The two books include links to numerous SEL competencies and domains and provide powerful questions to examine:

- **Self-awareness:** How did Priyanka identify and define her identity using experiences from her family's life in India and her present-day life in the United States?
- **Social awareness:** What aspects of social awareness, such as looking at things from the perspective of others and showing empathy and compassion, were demonstrated in these stories?
- **Relationship skills:** What conflicts did Marisol and Priyanja encounter in their journeys? How did they resolve them?

The themes and images of some of these books can be unfamiliar, difficult to understand, and frightening for young readers because of the books' representation of the hardships and mistreatment, especially when it is suffered by children. Some students may struggle to understand that experience and how they can relate to it. Bringing the concept of immigration and the experiences of new immigrants to the level of the classroom, school, and community can help students understand how such experiences can relate to their own lives. Exercises for the lesson can involve talking to students about new people in their community or school and the experiences that they are having adjusting to their new home. Students could talk about how they can offer a welcome and help for students navigating their new world, from finding new friends to adapting to changes in climate, food, games, and cultural activities. The lesson that change can begin with every individual, with small steps and good intentions, will support many SEL domains.

STEM

While STEM content, with an empirical focus and structure, may appear challenging to link to SEL themes, many SEL competencies in the areas of executive functioning and cognitive skills are a natural fit with STEM curricula. The Next Generation Science Standards include such topics as forces and ecosystems (third grade), Earth's place in the universe (fourth grade), Earth and human activity (fourth grade), engineering design (grades 3–5), and motion and stability (fifth grade). The images and text of graphic novels and illustrated texts provide a creative way to link together the STEM topic content with SEL competencies. Biographies of pioneering STEM leaders provide a wide variety of opportunities to look at SEL themes such as fostering perseverance, grit, and creativity; developing cognitive skills such as goal setting, task initiation, and time management; good decision-making; working through challenges and learning from failure; and building skills around self- and social awareness. The stories of important STEM events, discoveries, and inventions offer opportunities to link in SEL themes that are relevant to the events; for example, ingenuity, creativity, teamwork, conflict management, and time management have been crucial for the success of conservation and other environmental movements. A wide variety of books that show everyday people, including young people, using creativity, ingenuity, and perseverance to achieve their goals or complete a task are a great source of inspiration within the sciences.

Two graphic novels, *Saving Sorya: Chang and the Sun Bear* and *Saving H'Non: Chang and the Elephant,* by Trang Nguyen, a Vietnamese wildlife conservation scientist and environmental activist, tell the story of Trang's decision to become a conservationist and her meeting and rescue of an orphaned sun bear and an Asian elephant. The books tie together the scientific concepts about conservation with SEL themes of empathy and compassion, recognizing situational demands and opportunities, and reflecting on one's role to promote personal, family, and community well-being. The SEL themes that run through *Saving Sorya* and *Saving H'Non* include:

- **Self-awareness:** How did Trang's experiences help her develop a sense of purpose, and how was this shown in her actions?
- **Relationship skills:** How did Trang stand up for the rights and needs of Sorya and H'Non?
- **Responsible decision-making:** How did Trang demonstrate curiosity and open-mindedness? How did she view her role in helping the well-being of the animals?

A strong link between SEL themes and STEM content can also be found in the exercises and activities of the subjects. Completion of STEM activities requires cognitive skills, such as goal setting, task initiation, and time management as well as problem-solving and learning from failure. Group activities require the development and use of good communication skills among the students: dividing up roles and responsibilities, assigning tasks, meeting goals and deadlines, and providing support, encouragement, and understanding throughout the project, but especially during challenging periods. To supplement the activities, hands-on and how-to stories offer inspiring and humorous lessons to show how to approach and overcome challenges and accept failures.

A number of popular books that show examples of ingenuity and creativity provide wonderful opportunities for prompting creative brainstorming and inspiring hands-on activities, whether in a structured lesson or a more open maker-space setting. Series such as David Macauley's books, including the How It Works series, use clear and colorful diagrams and images to explain features of our world, from castles to toilets, jet planes, and eyes. The Big Ideas that Changed the World series by Don Brown includes such books as *A Shot in the Arm!*, which tells history of vaccinations, *Rocket to the Moon!*, *We the People!*, *All Charged Up!*, and *Machines That Think!* Macauley's and Brown's books inspire creativity and brainstorming, as well as SEL skills such as problem-solving, creative planning, and construction, prompting questions of "What if . . . ?", "How can I?", and "How does this work?"

The SEL themes that run through these stories include:

- **Cognitive:** What is a problem that my classroom/community is facing, and how can I address is? (These questions can tie in the scientific theories and discussion.) What materials will I need? How did the explorers or inventors of the books recognize the problem and come to a decision to solve it?
- **Self-management:** How did the explorers or inventors in the books manage their own emotions? How did they take initiative in deciding on her inventions? How can I set goals for myself to achieve a solution?
- **Responsible decision-making:** How did the explorers or inventors demonstrate good decision-making skills, like curiosity and open-mindedness? Did they consider the best way to achieve their goals before making decisions on how to proceed?

ELA

With the breadth of content of course material, there are innumerable opportunities to teach social and emotional learning within ELA, and the integration of illustrated texts into lessons is a natural step. CASEL, for example, published a guide to integrating each of their five core SEL competencies with elementary ELA instruction (2017), providing examples both of teaching SEL skills through the specific content and as general competencies in the exercises. For example, it suggests using ELA time to help foster self-awareness and self-management skills such as self-calming, focusing, and time management. Within the ELA content, CASEL suggests focusing on the SEL competency of social awareness by having students take the perspective of characters within stories and practicing empathy for their challenges, life experiences, and outlooks (CASEL, 2017).

The Elephants Come Home: A True Story of Seven Elephants, Two People, and One Extraordinary Friendship, written by Kim Tomsic and illustrated by Hadley Hooper, tells the true story of Lawrence and Françoise Anthony, who created a wildlife reserve in KwaZulu-Natal that became home to a herd of elephants. The story involves the death of the main, beloved character and examines the humans' and animals' responses. *The Elephants Come Home* is a lovely and moving book that serves as an excellent starting point for the sample lesson from CASEL (2017) and suggests activities such as identifying the characters' feelings, having the students discuss in small groups the influence of emotions on our actions, and talking about how characters' feelings and points of view affect others and the story's resolution. The SEL themes that run through the story include:

- **Emotion:** How do the elephants show their emotions throughout the book? How does the design of the book illustrate the moods and emotions of the animals?
- **Social awareness:** How does the book show the characters' (human and animal) capacity for compassion?
- **Self-management:** What were some examples of personal goals, planning, and organizational strategies that Lawrence and Françoise used?

Wordless Illustrated Texts

Using wordless books in ELA lessons creates opportunities for students to develop comprehension, vocabulary, and expression skills to understand and discuss the story in their own words. By placing the focus solely on the images in the book, children can see the importance of the images, with each child drawing on different views and aspects of the pictures to retell the story in their own words. Two beautifully illustrated texts that are largely or entirely wordless include *The Wanderer* by Peter van den Ende, which shows the journey of a small boat across great bodies of water, past sea monsters and schools of fish. It is a story of bravery, exploration, and discovery that can be interpreted in many ways and provides myriad starters for discussions in the classroom. *The Invention of Hugo Cabret* by Brian Selznick is a Caldecott Award-winning work that combines detailed drawings with text to tell the story of an orphaned boy living in the walls of a Paris train station, as he seeks to bring to life an automaton that his father left behind after his death. The creative use of images and limited or no text in the books highlight the power of the images and allow the authors to highlight emotions without describing them. Students can infer the characters' emotions and interpret their meanings through the images.

Cross-curricular lessons

The overlapping themes and topics of multiple core curricula allow for opportunities to integrate both subjects within a single lesson or across multiple periods of the day. Social studies does not have a prominent place within the curriculum of elementary classrooms, so cross-curricular connections help educators address that content more efficiently. Biographies of environmentalists and conservationists in STEM provide a natural link with the topic of advocacy movements in social studies. One example is *The Great Stink: How Joseph Bazalgette Solved London's Poop Problem,* written by Colleen Paeff and illustrated by Nancy Carpenter, which tells the story of the creation of the London sewer system in 1858, combining history and science with engaging illustrations and a postscript about water pollution and efforts to prevent it and the spread of waterborne diseases such as cholera.

Differentiation

There are multiple ways to differentiate lessons for students with a range of abilities and interests and in mixed-ability classrooms. One method is adding breadth in the content coverage by integrating additional books or materials with different viewpoints on the same general topic. The ability to select books with differing reading levels, topics, lengths, and diversity of viewpoint provides educators with rich opportunities for differentiating the lesson. In mixed-ability classrooms with advanced, at-level, and below-level students, the lessons can use a mixture of graphic books, including non-conforming books, wordless books, and high-low readers.

Building a Lesson Plan

The starting point of a lesson plan can be either the core subject content or the SEL theme, and from there the content and SEL theme can be linked through the selection of a book. For example, starting with a social studies unit on a historical figure or event, teachers can pull out SEL themes such as empathy, perspective, and identity, then create questions or activities around those SEL domains through a picture book in the topic. Starting with an SEL theme such as emotions or cognitive skills, teachers can build out a unit within one of the core subjects such as science or ELA, supported by a book. Later chapters in this book will give specific examples of building lessons with correlations to curricular standards in social studies, STEM, and ELA, with lists of leveled picture books divided by content topics and SEL themes and sample lesson plans. This section will provide a template of how to create a general differentiated lesson using picture books and SEL themes.

Teachers can start by selecting the content topic and relevant content standards. Table 4.2 lists the links to the relevant content standards for science, social studies, ELA, and STEM that teachers can consult when building the topic content and skills covered in the lesson plan.

Table 4.2 Selecting Subject Content and Standards for a Lesson Plan

Subject Content	Standards
Language Arts	Common Core English Language Arts—Informational text Common Core English Language Arts—Literature https://www.thecorestandards.org/ELA-Literacy
Social Studies	National Council for the Social Studies https://www.socialstudies.org/national-curriculum-standards-social-studies-chapter-2-themes-social-studies C3: https://www.socialstudies.org/standards/c3
Math	Common Core Mathematics https://www.thecorestandards.org/Math
Science	Next Generation Science Standards https://www.nextgenscience.org/search-standards
Technology	ISTE: https://www.iste.org/standards/iste-standards-for-students

Having selected the core topic and relevant standards, a teacher could select a book related to the topic. Table 4.3 provides questions to think about when selecting a book for the lesson. Factors to consider include the quality of the book, the difficulty level and length, how well it matches with the challenges and strengths of the students who will read it, and whether it represents a diverse viewpoint.

The final component to consider in building the lesson plan is the SEL domains and competencies that the teacher would like to cover in the lesson. Table 4.4 lists the CASEL competencies and gives examples of each.

Example: Building Out a Lesson Plan

As an example, to begin to build a lesson focusing on immigration, teachers could start with the appropriate standards for social studies—the C3 Framework, which are linked to the Common Core ELA Standards, or the National Council for the Social Studies (NCSS) Standards. These standards can also be linked to the ELA/Literacy Common Core Standards in areas such as reading, writing, and speaking and listening. C3 standards in

Table 4.3 Selecting a Picture Book for a Lesson Plan

Criteria	Considerations
Overall Quality	Is it a quality book? • Rich themes or central ideas • Multi-faceted characters or key individuals • Complex illustrations • Rich language • Multi-layered plot • Accurate (for informational texts) Do you like it? Are you excited to share the book with your students?
Topic & Theme Alignment	Does the topic align with the content area standards or serve as a base for the ELA standards? Does the theme align with the SEL domains or competencies you want to address?
Length	For a read-aloud, does the length match the attention span of the children in your classroom? For an independent or small-group read, does this book provide the needed challenge or support (i.e., a longer book can challenge a stronger reader and a shorter book can provide a more manageable task for a less-proficient reader)?
Complexity	Have you considered quantitative, qualitative, and reader and task factors to determine if the book is a good fit?
Diversity	Do the chosen books represent the children in your classroom? Do the chosen books represent the diversity in broader society? Do the authors of the chosen books represent different areas of diversity (e.g., race, class, gender, language, religion, dis/ability)?

the areas of geography support many aspects of a lesson around immigration, such as:

> **D2.Geo.7.3–5.** Explain how cultural and environmental characteristics affect the distribution and movement of people, goods, and ideas.
> **D2.Geo.4.3–5.** Explain how culture influences the way people modify and adapt to their environments.
> **D2.Geo.6.3–5.** Describe how environmental and cultural characteristics influence population distribution in specific places or regions.

Table 4.4 Selecting SEL Domains and Competencies for a Lesson Plan

CASEL Competencies https://casel.org/sel-framework	Examples
Self management	• Managing emotions • Using self-discipline • Taking initiative • Demonstrating agency • Using planning and organizational skills
Self-awareness	• Identifying emotions • Examining prejudices and biases • Developing interests and a sense of purpose • Having a growth mindset
Social awareness	• Taking other people's perspectives • Demonstrating empathy, compassion, and gratitude • Identifying diverse social norms, including unjust ones
Responsible decision-making	• Evaluating personal, interpersonal, community, and institutional impacts • Reflecting on one's role to promote personal, family, and community well-being • Demonstrating curiosity and open-mindedness • Identifying solutions for personal and social problems
Relationship skills	• Communicating effectively • Demonstrating cultural competency

Sources: CASEL (2020). www.casel.org/what-is-SEL

Teachers can then select a book that is appropriate for the class on the topic of immigration. In addition to considering the questions in Table 4.2, publisher and reviewer websites such as Kirkus (free), *School Library Journal*, and *Publishers Weekly* (both fee-based) provide helpful reviews of elementary-level books that indicate target age level and the quality of the book; starred reviews from any of those three sites are reliable indications that the book is high quality. School librarians are also an excellent source of advice for quality picture books for certain groups of students on specific topics. A book's page on Amazon will often list excerpts from the three publishers and indicate if the publishers gave the book a starred review in the Editorial Reviews section.

The selection of multiple books with varying reading levels, length, and focus offers an excellent opportunity to create a differentiated lesson plan, especially for a class with a range of reading abilities. In the small-group or individual work portion of the lesson, a selection of books can be shared with the students and then discussed. This allows students to contribute information from multiple perspectives with everyone having a reading experience that is tailored to their needs and abilities.

As a last step, teachers can consider the SEL themes that are highlighted both in the subject content of immigration and in the books that will be used in the lesson. The plot points, illustrations, and dialogue of picture books about immigration movements offer many entry points to SEL domains and competencies, including values, perspectives, identity, social awareness, and responsible decision-making. Biographies of leaders in immigration movements will demonstrate such characteristics as courage, hope, grit, and perseverance, as well self-management and responsible decision-making. Books that discuss the historical events will address social awareness aspects, such as identifying diverse social norms, including unjust ones.

Assessments and rubrics can incorporate various aspects of the lesson component, including the SEL portions, the book reading, and the subject content. Informal assessments can look at students' participation in the discussions, completion of the activities, and their work on any individual or small-group assignments, such as writing pieces, presentations, and artistic creations.

The next three chapters will focus on each of the three core subject areas: STEM, social studies, and ELA, with details of the main national curriculum standards, relevant SEL domains and competencies, suggested graphic novels or illustrated texts, and a sample lesson plan.

References

CASEL. (2017). *Examples of social and emotional learning in elementary English Language Arts instruction.* https://casel.org/sel-in-elementary-ela-8-20-17

CASEL. (2020). *CASEL'S SEL Framework: What are the core competence areas and where are they promoted?* www.casel.org/what-is-SEL

National Council for the Social Studies (NCSS). (2013). *The College, Career, and Civic Life (C3) Framework for Social Studies State Standards: Guidance for enhancing the rigor of K-12 civics, economics, geography, and history.* NCSS.

National Governors Association Center for Best Practices & Council of Chief State School Officers (NGACBP & CCSS). (2010). *Common Core State Standards for English Language Arts and Literacy in History/Social Studies, Science, and Technical Subjects.* Authors. www.corestandards.org/wp-content/uploads/ELA_Standards.pdf

National Governors Association Center for Best Practices & Council of Chief State School Officers (NGACBP & CCSS). (2010). *Common Core State Standards for mathematics.* Authors. https://www.thecorestandards.org/wp-content/uploads/Math_Standards1

Book List

Brown, D. (2019). *Rocket to the moon! Big ideas that changed the world.* Abrams Fanfare.

Brown, D. (2020). *Machines that think! Big ideas that changed the world.* Abrams Fanfare.

Brown, D. (2021). *A Shot in the arm! Big ideas that changed the world.* Abrams Fanfare.

Brown, D. (2022). *We the people! Big ideas that changed the world.* Abrams Fanfare.

Brown, D. (2024). *All charged up! Big ideas that changed the world.* Abrams Fanfare.

Castellanos, A. (2022). *Isla to island.* Atheneum Books for Young Readers.

Chanani, N. (2017). *Pashmina.* Macmillan.

Jamieson, V., Mohamed, O., & Geddy, I. (2020). *When stars are scattered.* Dial Books for Young Readers.

Macauley, D. (2015a). *Eye: How it works.* Square Fish.

Macauley, D. (2015b). *Jet plane: How it works.* Square Fish.

Macauley, D. (2015c). *Toilet: How it works.* Square Fish.

Nguyen, T. (2021). *Saving Sorya: Chang and the Sun Bear* (J. Zdung, Illus.). Penguin Random House.

Nguyen, T. (2023). *Saving H'Non: Chang and the elephant* (J. Zdung, Illus.). Penguin Random House.

Paeff, C. (2021). *The great stink: How Joseph Bazalgette solved London's poop problem* (N. Carpenter, Illus.). Margaret K. McElderry Books.
Selznick, B. (2015). *The invention of Hugo Cabret*. Scholastic Press.
Tomsic, K. (2021). *The elephants come home: A true story of seven elephants, two people, and one extraordinary friendship* (H. Hooper, Illus.). Chronicle Books.
van den Ende, P. (2020). *The Wanderer*. Levine Querido.

5

Integrating SEL and STEM

I received a high-tech book light as a Christmas present this year. It was sitting on my desk, out of its box, and a second-grader, Orla, picked it up and examined it. "What's this?," she asked curiously. I replied with my typical silliness, "It's my new electric toothbrush." Orla looked at me suspiciously and immediately went into inquiry and discovery mode. She picked up the sleek, sky blue light, which resembles a pocket-sized robot, and snapped open the metal clasp for holding it in place on a book. She fiddled with the row of buttons that turn the light off and on and adjust the brightness and color of the light, and swiveled the small light at the top that can be twisted and angled in all directions for maximum illumination. I could see Orla's brain working through the possibilities of what this little gadget was. "Not a toothbrush," she said at last, with a delighted smile, "A book light!"

This process of inquiry is common for children from the youngest ages—putting objects into their mouths, dropping them repeatedly from highchairs, testing properties of magnetism, seeing what floats and what sinks, and using many other methods to figure out the purpose and attributes of an object. Children discover and define their world through forms of inquiry that include questions, tactile examinations, empirical investigations, and informal explorations.

The use of inquiry-based learning is especially important in the areas of science, technology, engineering, and math (STEM).

FIGURES 5.1 and **5.2** These pages from the first book in Jon Scieszka's Astronuts series, *Mission One: The Plant Planet*, show examples of the series' humorous and engaging text and graphics.

The National Research Council of America recommended the incorporation of inquiry into the STEM curriculum, calling it a "critical component of a science program at all grade levels and in every domain of science" (Ireland et al., 2012, p. 160). The use

FIGURES 5.1 and **5.2** (*Continued*)

of inquiry allows students to create hypotheses, gather data, analyze results, and make arguments and conclusions. In addition to the focus on the STEM content, inquiry-based pedagogies support the development of SEL skills, such as critical thinking and strong decision-making, and social regulation skills, such as communication and collaboration, in the areas of executive functioning and meta-cognition (Dobber et al., 2017).

The SEL curriculum is a valuable way to teach and foster inquiry because it helps students learn to appropriately formulate, ask, and respond to questions, which is vital to STEM learning. Illustrated texts on STEM topics for readers in the upper elementary grades provide a valuable bridge between STEM content and SEL competencies, offering rich and varied opportunities for students to explore scientific themes and concepts while incorporating inquiry-based learning and SEL skills. Fiction and non-fiction STEM-related texts offer examples of using questions to explore, define, and even challenge aspects of the world. A great example is the AstroNuts series by Jon Scieszka, in which the adventures of four "superpowered animal astronauts" who go on exploratory missions from NNASA (Not the National Aeronautics and Space Administration) are described. In the first book in the series, *Mission One: The Plant Planet*, the crew describes the critical rise in carbon dioxide levels on Earth and sets out to find a new planet that would support life on Earth (see Figures 5.1 and 5.2).

Through the characters, plotlines, and illustrations of these books, students can generate and answer key questions, such as:

- How and why do things work the way they do?
- How and why have changes occurred?
- What work did this scientist do, and how did it change the world?
- How did this discovery, invention, or development change our planet and the way we interact with it?

This chapter will address three main areas of STEM: science, mathematics, and technology, using the standards for each subject: the Common Core Standards for Math, the Next Generation Science Standards, and the technology standards from the International Society for Technology in Education (ISTE). With each set of correlations, we will show examples of links between the standards and SEL domains and will provide examples of specific texts. The chapter concludes with a sample lesson plan.

Science

The Next Generation Science Standards require students to ask questions, develop and use models, plan and carry out investigations, analyze and interpret data, engage in argument using evidence, and obtain, evaluate, and communicate information (NGSS Lead States, 2013). These capabilities and aptitudes require students to develop skill sets that fall into SEL competencies such as self-awareness, self-management, and responsible decision-making. Table 5.1 provides examples of correlations between the NGSS and SEL competencies that can be incorporated in lessons and exercises.

Table 5.1 Sample NGSS and Related SEL Competencies

Grade	Sample NGSS Performance Expectations	SEL Competencies
Third Grade	• Define problems • Plan and carry out investigations • Engage in argument from evidence • Obtain, evaluate, and communicate information	**Self-awareness:** Experiencing self-efficacy; developing interests and a sense of purpose **Self-management:** Setting personal and collective goals
Fourth Grade	• Demonstrate grade-appropriate proficiency in asking questions • Analyze and interpret data • Construct explanations and design solutions • Obtain, evaluate, and communicate information	**Responsible decision-making:** Recognizing how critical thinking skills are useful both inside and outside school **Self-management:** Using planning and organizational skills
Fifth Grade	• Develop and use models • Plan and carry out investigations • Obtain, evaluate, and communicate information • Demonstrate understanding of the core ideas	**Relationship skills:** Communicating effectively **Responsible decision-making:** Learning how to make a reasoned judgment after analyzing information, data, and facts

Source: NGSS Lead States (2013).

The NGSS Standards are also correlated to the Common Core Standards for LA/Literacy, which work well with illustrated texts on a wide variety of STEM topics and offer opportunities for cross-curricular lessons that address multiple subjects. Examples of relevant Common Core Standards include:

- "Ask and answer questions to demonstrate understanding of a text, referring explicitly to the text as the basis for the answers" (CCSS.ELA-Literacy.RI.3.1)
- "Describe the relationship between a series of historical events, scientific ideas or concepts, or steps in technical procedures in a text, using language that pertains to time, sequence, and cause/effect" (CCSS.ELA-Literacy.RI.3.3)
- "Explain how an author uses reasons and evidence to support particular points in a text." (CCSS.ELA-Literacy.RI.4.8)

Math

The Common Core Standards for Mathematics are broken into two categories: standards for mathematical practice and standards for mathematical content. The standards for practice are based on learning processes and proficiencies that are considered vital for students to be successful, many of which support core SEL domains. Table 5.2 provides examples of correlations between the Common Core Standards for math practice and SEL domains that can be incorporated in lessons and exercises.

Technology

ISTE offers technology standards for students in K-12. Table 5.3 lists the seven broad categories of standards with examples of specific outcomes and correlated SEL themes and domains.

Table 5.2 Sample Common Core Standards for Mathematics and Related SEL Competencies

Common Core Standards for Mathematical Practice	SEL Competencies
• Make sense of problems and persevere in solving them	**Self-awareness:** Experiencing self-efficacy **Self-management:** Setting personal and collective goals; using planning and organizational skills
• Construct viable arguments and critique the reasoning of others	**Relationship skills:** Communicating effectively; practicing teamwork and collaborative problem-solving **Self-awareness:** Having a growth mindset
• Use appropriate tools strategically • Attend to precision	**Social awareness:** Recognizing situational demands and opportunities **Responsible decision-making:** Learning how to make a reasoned judgment after analyzing information, data, and facts; identifying solutions for personal and social problems; recognizing how critical thinking skills are useful both inside and outside school

Source: National Governors Association Center for Best Practices, Council of Chief State School Officers (2010).

Table 5.3 Sample Standards for Technology and Related SEL Competencies

ISTE Standard	Sample Outcomes	SEL Competencies
Empowered Learner	• Students articulate and set personal learning goals, develop strategies leveraging technology to achieve them and reflect on the learning process itself to improve learning outcomes. • Students build networks and customize their learning environments in ways that support the learning process.	**Self-management:** Goal-setting, using planning and organizational skills **Self-awareness:** Identifying personal, cultural, and linguistic assets; experiencing self-efficacy; developing interests and a sense of purpose

(Continued)

Table 5.3 (Continued)

ISTE Standard	Sample Outcomes	SEL Competencies
Digital Citizen	• Students cultivate and manage their digital identity and reputation and are aware of the permanence of their actions in the digital world. • Students engage in positive, safe, legal and ethical behavior when using technology • Students demonstrate an understanding of and respect for the rights and obligations of using and sharing intellectual property	**Self-awareness:** Demonstrating honesty and integrity **Self-management:** Demonstrating personal and collective agency **Responsible decision-making:** Anticipating and evaluating the consequences of one's actions
Knowledge Constructor	• Students build knowledge by actively exploring real-world issues and problems, developing ideas and theories and pursuing answers and solutions	**Social awareness:** Recognizing situational demands and opportunities; understanding the influences of organizations and systems on behavior **Responsible decision-making:** Identifying solutions for personal and social problems; recognizing how critical thinking skills are useful both inside and outside school
Innovative Designer	• Students exhibit a tolerance for ambiguity, perseverance, and the capacity to work with open-ended problems.	**Self-awareness:** Having a growth mindset; developing interests and a sense of purpose
Computational Thinker	• Students collect data or identify relevant data sets, use digital tools to analyze them, and represent data in various ways to facilitate problem-solving and decision-making. • Students break problems into component parts, extract key information, and develop descriptive models to understand complex systems or facilitate problem-solving.	**Responsible decision-making:** Learning how to make a reasoned judgment after analyzing information, data, and facts

ISTE Standard	Sample Outcomes	SEL Competencies
Creative Communicator	• Students communicate complex ideas clearly and effectively by creating or using a variety of digital objects.	**Relationship skills:** Communicating effectively **Responsible decision-making:** Learning how to make a reasoned judgment after analyzing information, data, and facts
Global Collaborator	• Students use digital tools to connect with learners from a variety of backgrounds and cultures, engaging with them in ways that broaden mutual understanding and learning. • Students use collaborative technologies to work with others, including peers, experts or community members, to examine issues and problems from multiple viewpoints. • Students contribute constructively to project teams, assuming various roles and responsibilities to work effectively toward a common goal. • Students explore local and global issues and use collaborative technologies to work with others to investigate solutions.	**Self-awareness:** Integrating personal and social identities **Social awareness:** Taking others' perspectives; demonstrating empathy and compassion; recognizing strengths in others **Relationship skills:** Communicating effectively; practicing teamwork and collaborative problem-solving; showing leadership in groups; seeking or offering support and help when needed

Source: International Society for Technology in Education (2000).

Graphic Novels and Illustrated Texts in STEM

STEM-themed graphic novels and illustrated texts for grades 3–5 can be loosely grouped into three categories: 1) books that focus on characters asking questions, exploring and investigating, and finding answers; 2) descriptions of "Big Ideas" and how things work, often narrated by unusual animals, peoples, or creatures; and 3) biographical and historical accounts of inspiring figures and events in STEM fields. The images in these books supplement the text not only by illustrating the key concepts described in the text but by offering visual examples of data collection and presentation in colorful and often funny graphics.

Questions and Investigations

There are many outstanding individual books and book series that feature characters asking STEM-related questions and

FIGURES 5.3 and **5.4** These pages from Jon Scieszka's *Mission One: The Plant Planet* offer examples of the series' realistic logs, worksheets, and other research templates.

Integrating SEL and STEM ♦ 81

investigating to find answers. *Jop and Blip Wanna Know . . . Can You Hear a Penguin Fart on Mars? And Other Excellent Questions* by Jim Benton asks a series of scientific questions and provides witty and offbeat explanations, including the answer to the title question, which is "maybe" (but the noise will be muted by the thin atmosphere on Mars). The Stick and Stone graphic

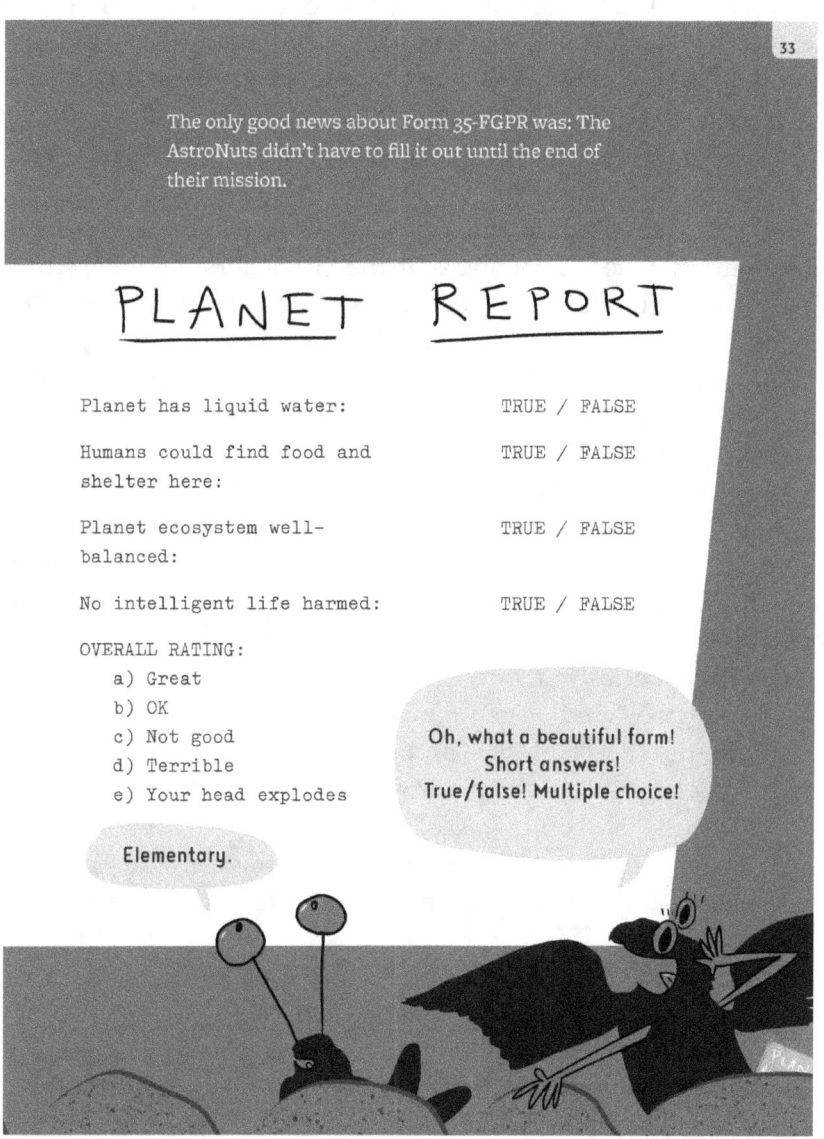

FIGURES 5.3 and **5.4** (*Continued*)

novel series (a companion to the Stick and Stone picture books), written by Beth Ferry and illustrated by Kristen Cella, has two books so far: *Stick and Stone Explore and More* and *Stick and Stone on the Go*. The second book has two stories, with an activity for each. In the first story, Stick and Stone explore a cave, and an activity on creating cave art follows the story. In the second story, Stick and Stone seek to find a good pet and decide on a caterpillar, which then metamorphosizes into a butterfly. The concluding activity for the story has children create a stick and leaf butterfly.

The Noodleheads series, written by Tedd Arnold, Martha Hamilton, and Mitch Weiss, introduces a pair of pasta pieces, Mac and Mac, who ask questions about how the world works. The author's note explains that the characters were based on the terms "noodles" or "noodleheads," a reference to an 1888 book by W. A. Clouston that referred to stories dating back millennia that focused on the adventures of foolish characters. "Noodlehead stories . . . help children understand humor, logical thinking, and the importance of distinguishing between what's true and what's a lie" (no page number). In *Noodleheads Do the Impossible*, the sixth book in the series, Mac and Mac set out to count the stars in the sky and the grains of sand on Earth. The books offer a joyful view of asking questions and discovery and emphasize the view that there is no such thing as a "stupid question."

Many books in this genre give examples of scientific studies, with sample charts, graphs, and questions embedded in the plot of the book while also being provided as templates for activities for the students. For example, *Astronuts Misson One: The Plant Planet* includes many of the reports that the astronuts need to complete during their search for an inhabitable planet (see Figure 5.2).

This subgenre of STEM graphic novels and illustrated texts supports many SEL competencies, especially in the areas of executive functioning and cognitive development. Examples of cooperation, communication, problem-solving, and managing failure are all demonstrated by characters as they set out on their explorations. Teachers can use the narrative, characters' actions, and illustrations to ask such questions as:

Self-management:

- How did the characters work together or alone to set personal and collective goals?
- What is an example of the characters using planning and organizational skills?
- How did the characters show the courage to take initiative?

Responsible decision-making:

- Give an example of the characters demonstrating curiosity and open-mindedness.
- Describe a point in the book in which the characters make a reasoned judgment after analyzing information, data, and facts.

Big Ideas

A subgenre of STEM-related graphic novels and illustrated texts that is similar to the books of questions and investigations are the books that have one or more characters explain a "Big Idea," such as the scientific history of an object or phenomenon. *Oliver's Great Big Universe* by Jorge Cham follows the adventures of 11-year-old Max, who eagerly explains scientific concepts ranging from black holes to ghost particles to why Mercury resembles a meatball from the lunchroom cafeteria. *Older Than Dirt* by Don Brown and Mike Perfit offers a concise and humorous history of Earth, from the Big Bang to the eventual demise of the Sun, as told by a groundhog and a worm. Mike Barfield and Jess Bradley's A Day in the Life series includes *A Day in the Life of a Poo, a Gnu, and You* as well as *A Day in the Life of An Astronaut, Mars, and the Distant Stars*. The vivid illustrations, easy-to-understand explanations, and charming humor make these books irresistible to curious young readers and adults alike. With explanations in small segments of one or two pages, the book can easily be read for short periods or referred to for specific topics and explanations. The colorful illustrations also offer an excellent example of a multimedia project that teachers can build for their students.

Related to this subgenre are book series that directly teach STEM subject content through the characters' adventures. Jon Chad's graphic novel series The Solvers teaches readers aged 8 and up foundational math skills as the characters fight crime and battle the evil Null Void. *Everything Awesome About Sharks and Other Underwater Creatures,* written and illustrated by Mike Lowery, is an example of a topic-specific text with engaging illustrations and a wealth of information about oceans, sharks, and other deep-sea habitats and animals. The book's bonus materials include instructions for drawing various sea creatures and a collection of "deep sea jokes":

> What does seaweed yell when it's in danger?
> "Kelp!"
>
> What does an angler fish write in her journal?
> Deep thoughts!

For older or more advanced readers, Don Brown's illustrated texts *Drowned City: Hurricane Katrina and New Orleans* and *The Great American Dustbowl* are powerful graphic novels that explain the stories of the two natural disasters and their impact on the people living through them, offering an excellent opportunity for a cross-curricular lesson that combines science and social studies topics.

This subgenre of STEM graphic novels and illustrated texts supports executive functioning and cognitive development as well as other SEL competencies. Teachers can use the narrative, characters' actions, and illustrations to ask such questions as:

Relationship skills:

- Did the characters communicate effectively or ineffectively? How?
- Describe an example when the characters practiced teamwork and collaborative problem-solving.
- How did the characters resolve conflicts?

Social awareness:

- How did the characters take (or reject) others' perspectives?
- Describe an example of a character recognizing situational demands and opportunities.
- How does this book demonstrate the influences of organizations and systems on behavior?

Biographical and Fictionalized Accounts of STEM Leaders and Events

Several series and individual books stand out as exceptional examples of illustrated texts that tell the stories of the inspiring work and lives of inventors, explorers, scientists, and other leaders in the STEM field, as well as descriptions of historical events in the that field. The GraphicScience Biographies series offers concise, colorfully illustrated stories of the life events of the books' subjects, along with a timeline and further resources. *Mary Anning and the Great Fossil Discoveries* by Jordi Bayarri tells of the life and discoveries of the paleontologist and fossil collector Mary Anning. Other subjects in the GraphicScience Biographies series include Marie Curie, Albert Einstein, Charles Darwin, Isaac Newton, Avicenna, Ada Lovelace, Galileo, and Louis Pasteur.

Torben Kuhlmann's gorgeously illustrated, fantastical tales about a little mouse who interacts with some of the most famous figures in history—Albert Einstein, Charles Lindbergh, Neil Armstrong, and Thomas Edison—offer beautiful renditions of the life and times of groundbreaking scientists, told from the point of view of an adventurous mouse. In *Einstein—The Fantastic Journey of a Mouse Through Space and Time*, the mouse creates a time machine to travel back and give Einstein the idea for the theory of relativity. In *Armstrong: The Adventurous Journey of a Mouse to the Moon*, the little mouse sets out to find out once and for all if the moon is indeed made of cheese. The book's accompanying materials include a summary of the history of space travel, starting with Galileo's observations. The characters' thoughts, observations, and decisions are excellent examples and good starting points for discussions about self-discipline, self-motivation, courage, initiative, and collective agency.

The Way of the Hive: A Honey Bee's Story by Jay Hosler describes and illustrates in detailed panels and text the evolution of the honey bee as told from the points of view of two honey bees, Nyuki and Dvorah. In one series of panels, Dvorah, a worker bee, caps Nyuki's cell so that the larva can go through metamorphosis, as she explains to Nyuki:

> Dvorah: Are you hungry now?
> Nyuki: Uh . . .
> Dvorah: You aren't, are you? Do you know why? Your weight has increased **2,000 times** in your five days as a larva. You've had to eat so much because your body needs a ton of energy for the metamorphosis. The fact that you're ***not*** hungry anymore means your body is ready for the change.

At the end of the book, Nyuki's and Dvorah's lives end, and their bodies are returned to the soil, where they feed the roots of new flowers. The book's afterword includes detailed illustrations of the anatomy of a bee, detailed annotations by the author about the illustrations, text, and scientific details behind the story. The bees reflect on Nyuki's and Dvorah's lives and their contributions to their community, which can prompt a rich discussion starting with questions such as:

- How did Nyuki and Dvorah understand their contributions to the other bees and the flowers?
- What feelings did Nyuki and Dvorah experience throughout their life cycles?
- How did Nyuki and Dvorah show the courage to take initiative?
- How did Nyuki and Dvorah show concern for the feelings of others and demonstrate empathy and compassion?

The Miracle Seed by Martin Lemelman tells the true story of Israeli doctor Sarah Sallon's work to grow an ancient date palm plant that went extinct about 2,000 years ago in what is now Israel, using seeds found in ancient burial sites. Weaving historical details with a botany lesson and examples of creative problem-solving and working through failure, the book combines SEL themes with a gripping scientific narrative. The history of the land and its conflicts at the time of the palm's extinction, combined with the efforts of Sarah Sallon in conjunction with the other archaeologists and botanists, offers a great range of SEL domains to highlight and discuss, including setting personal goals, using planning and organizational skills, demonstrating cooperation and teamwork, and having a growth mindset.

Though the STEM subjects seem at first to be too technical to fit easily into illustrated texts with SEL focuses, the core topics of the books dovetail well with many SEL domains. Scientific explanations, challenges, and discoveries are woven through many illustrated texts, whether they are topic-specific or books that address questions in nature, scientific themes, and Big Ideas. The graphic format provides excellent demonstrations and illustrations of the content and concepts described in the books while providing engaging and compelling examples of STEM characters, fictional or historical. These books support powerful lessons on such topics as creativity, overcoming adversity and facing failures, and cognitive skills.

LESSON PLAN

Title and Grade
The Way of the Hive: Exploring the Life of a Bee Grades: 4–5
Standards and Learning Objectives
Next Generation Science Standards • 4-LS1–1. Construct an argument that plants and animals have internal and external structures that function to support survival, growth, behavior, and reproduction. • 4-LS1–2. Use a model to describe that animals receive different types of information through their senses, process the information in their brain, and respond to the information in different ways. **Common Core Standards for ELA: Informational Text** • CCSS.ELA-Literacy.RI.3.1 Ask and answer questions to demonstrate understanding of a text, referring explicitly to the text as the basis for the answers. • CCSS.ELA-Literacy.RI.3.7 Use information gained from illustrations (e.g., maps, photographs) and the words in a text to demonstrate understanding of the text (e.g., where, when, why, and how key events occur). • CCSS.ELA-Literacy.RI.4.3 Explain events, procedures, ideas, or concepts in a historical, scientific, or technical text, including what happened and why, based on specific information in the text. **SEL Standard: CASEL** • Responsible decision-making: Learning how to make a reasoned judgment after analyzing information, data, and facts. • Self-awareness: Developing interest and a sense of purpose. • Self-management: Showing the courage to take initiative; demonstrating personal and collective agency.

Learning Objectives

After reading *The Way of the Hive*, students will prepare multimedia presentations or illustrated narrative pieces showing the life cycle of a bee, the threats to bees, and how we can help support bees.

ASSESSMENT

Informal assessments will include assessments of students' participation in whole and small group discussions and completion of the daily activities. Assessments will vary based on the level of the students; a suggested differentiated assessment would be that students' narrative pieces should be assessed formally using a rubric that includes key criteria such as:
- Organization
- Presentation of scientific information with correct citation format
- Language and vocabulary
- Use of images to support the text

LEARNING PLAN

Instructional Resources and Materials

- *The Way of the Hive* by Jay Hosler
- Video of author's reading: https://www.youtube.com/watch?v=F5JeZxUJOzk
- Butcher paper or large sheets of paper for a mural or multi-paneled picture
- Supplemental materials on the life cycle of a bee, threats to the bee population, and conservation efforts (see the reference list at the end of this lesson plan for some suggested sources)
- Presentation media, as available: paper, computer with PowerPoint, audio or video recording hardware
- Research materials

Daily Plans

Phase 1: Group Activity (1 Day)
The Way of the Hive is a long and visually complex book that will take several class periods to read in a whole-group setting. Selecting sections to share in a whole group or small groups would work well.

As an introductory discussion, ask small groups of students to think about the roles that bees play in our environment and world.
- What are some different types of bees?
- What do bees do to help plants and flowers grow?
- What happens when there are no bees in a garden?
- What are some threats to bees or causes for their diminishing populations?
- What can we do to help bees flourish?

Phase 2: Read-Aloud and Activities (2 –Days)
Using the CROWD strategy or another format to guide your development of discussion questions, ask students a variety of questions that allow them to develop their understanding of the key points in the text, including those that are directly stated and those that must be inferred.
- **Completion:** Nyuki and Dvorah were _____.
- **Recall:** How did Dvorah help Nyuki?
- **Open-ended:** What kind of challenges or dangers did Dvorah and Nyuki face?
- **W's:** Who were some of the other insects that Dvorah and Nyuki met? What were some of the jobs and responsibilities that Dvorah and Nyuki had? Where did Dvorah and Nyuki live? When did the story begin? Why did Melissa take Bloomington's pollen back to the hive?
- **Distancing:** What have you heard about in the news regarding efforts to protect bees? What other books have we read that show people trying to make a difference in environmental ways? What are some things you could do to help bees?

Phase 3: Differentiated Learning (3–4 Days—1½ Days per Project)
Learners' individual needs will be met through differentiation of content, process, and product. Activities can be individually focused or completed in small groups.

Group projects (these can be assigned or students can select a version):
1. Divide the stories into small narrative arcs and give them to small groups. Students will draw a mural or multi-paneled picture showing part of the story arc, characters, and settings.
2. Using information from the texts and with additional assistance as needed, students in teams will research the dangers facing bees and what we can do to save the Earth's bee population. Each team will create a presentation in the form of a drawing, spoken presentation, or PowerPoint.

Individual Activities
Level 1: Students will identify the life stages of a bee using the text and images from the book and present them in a multimedia format. (Use this opportunity to teach the technology skills needed as well, including basic audio/video recording, PowerPoint, or Google Slides.)
Level 2: Create a presentation showing the causes of the decline of bees, the effect of the bees' decline, and what needs to be done to save them. Which type of bees are endangered? Which are not?
Level 3: Students will research and write a biography of an environmentalist, conservationist, or movement, then will compare the details with those of the efforts to help save the bees.

Phase 4: Revisit Group Activity (1 Day)
On the first day, students were introduced to life cycles and threats to bees. On this final day, students can reflect back on two aspects of the lesson: the importance of bees and how we can save them. Students should share their work with the

whole class. The lesson can end with the group making a plan for helping bees in their community through such projects as knowledge sharing (e.g., designing and posting signs or posters in community places; doing presentations at science fairs or other assemblies) and actions in local and community areas, such as planting plants that are good homes and sources of food for pollinators.

References

Buchmann, S. (201). *Honey Bees: Letters from the Hive.* Ember.
Burns, L. (2022). *Honeybee Rescue: A Backyard Drama.* Charlesbridge.
Fleming, C. (2023). *Honeybee: The Busy Life of Apis Mellifera* (E. Rohmann, Illus.). Neal Porter Books.
Holasová, A.F. (2021). *Bruno the Beekeeper: A Honey Primer.* Candlewick.
Hosler, J. (2021). *The Way of the Hive: A Honey Bee's Story.* HarperAlley.
Slade, S. (2010). *What If There Were No Bees?: A Book About the Grassland Ecosystem* (C. Schwartz, Illus.). Picture Window Books.
Socha, P. (2017). *Bees: A Honeyed History.* Abrams Books.

References

Dobber, M., Zwart, R., Tanis, M., & van Oers, B. (2017). Literature review: The role of the teacher in inquiry-based education. *Educational Research Review, 22*(1): 194–214. https://doi.org/10.1016/j.edurev.2017.09.002

International Society for Technology in Education. (2000). *ISTE National Educational Technology Standards* (NETS). Eugene, OR. https://www.iste.org/standards/iste-standards-for-students

Ireland, J. E., Watters, J. J., Brownlee, J., & Lupton, M. (2012). Elementary teacher's conceptions of inquiry teaching: Messages for teacher development. *Journal of Science Teacher Education,* 23(2): 159–175. https://doi.org/10.1007/s10972-011-9251-2

National Governors Association Center for Best Practices & Council of Chief State School Officers (NGACBP & CCSS). (2010). *Common Core State Standards: Mathematics Standards.* Authors.

Next Generation Science Standards (NGSS) Lead States. (2013). *Next Generation Science Standards: For states, by states.* The National Academies Press. https://www.nextgenscience.org/search-standards

Book List

Arnold, T., Hamilton, M., & Weiss, M. (2016–2023). *The Noodleheads* (Vols. 1–7) (T. Arnold, Illus.). Holiday House.

Arnold, T., Hamilton, M., & Weiss, M. (2021). *Noodleheads do the impossible* (T. Arnold, Illus.). Holiday House.

Barfield, M. & Bradley, J. (2021). *A day in the life of an astronaut, Mars, and the distant stars.* Aladdin.

Barfield, M. & Bradley, J. (2023). *A day in the life of a poo, a gnu, and you.* Aladdin.

Bayarri, J. (2023). *Mary Anning and the great fossil discoveries* (J. Bayarri, Illus.). Graphic Universe.

Benton, J. (2021). *Jop and Blip wanna know … can you hear a penguin fart on Mars? And other excellent questions.* HarperAlley.

Brown, D. (2015). *Drowned city: Hurricane Katrina and New Orleans.* Clarion Books.

Brown, D. (2017). *The Great American Dustbowl.* Clarion Books.

Brown, D. & Perfit, M. (2017). *Older than dirt: A wild but true history of Earth* (D. Brown, Illus.). Clarion Books.

Cham, J. (2023). *Oliver's great big universe.* Abrams Books.

Dolz, J. B. (2020–2023). *Graphic science biographies* (Vols. 1–9). Graphic Universe.

Ferry, B. (2022). *Stick and Stone explore and more* (K. Cella, Illus.). Clarion Books.

Ferry, B. (2023). *Stick and Stone on the go* (K. Cella, Illus.). Clarion Books.

Hosler, J. (2021). *The way of the hive: A honey bee's story.* HarperAlley.

Kuhlmann, T. (2014). *Lindbergh: The tale of a flying mouse* (D. H. Wilson, Trans.). NorthSouth Books.

Kuhlmann, T. (2016). *Armstrong: The adventurous journey of a mouse to the moon* (D. H. Wilson, Trans.). NorthSouth Books.

Kuhlmann, T. (2018). *Edison: The mystery of the missing mouse treasure* (D. H. Wilson, Trans.). NorthSouth Books.

Kuhlmann, T. (2021). *Einstein: The fantastic journey of a mouse through space and time* (D. H. Wilson, Trans.). NorthSouth Books.

Lemelman, M. (2023). *The miracle seed.* Eerdmans Books for Young Readers.

Lowery, M. (2019). *Everything awesome about dinosaurs and other prehistoric beasts!* Orchard Books.

Lowery, M. (2020). *Everything awesome about sharks and other underwater creatures!* Orchard Books.

Lowery, M. (2021). *Everything awesome about space and other galactic facts!* Orchard Books.
Scieszka, J. (2019). *AstroNuts Mission One: The plant planet* (S. Weinberg, Illus.). Chronicle Books.
Scieszka, J. (2020). *AstroNuts Mission Two: The water planet* (S. Weinberg, Illus.). Chronicle Books.
Scieszka, J. (2021). *AstroNuts Mission Three: The perfect planet* (S. Weinberg, Illus.). Chronicle Books.

6
Integrating SEL and Social Studies

Just as students seek to discover and explain the scientific world through inquiry and exploration, children and young students explore their place in the world by asking a multitude of questions and using the information they gather to help them define and forge their own identities. Curricula and pedagogy in a variety of subjects help students understand their own and others' racial, ethnic, gender, and cultural identities. Themes in social studies curricula touch on differences and similarities of people and how and why groups of people move around the world and shape history. Through a variety of media and narratives, from autobiographies to historical fiction, maps, art and artifacts, and news accounts, students can learn how they came to be the people they are and envision where they might go next. The graphic format of the books allows the authors and illustrators to use images, color, and presentation of the text to give multiple meanings to the storylines or narratives.

There are two key sets of standards for social studies: the College, Career, and Civic Life (C3) Framework for Social Studies and the National Council for Social Studies (NCSS) Standards. These standards overlap and can be integrated with each other, and they can also be correlated to Common Core standards, including the Common Core standards for English Language, specifically anchor standards Reading 1–10; Writing 1, 7–9; Speaking and Listening 1–6; Language 6, and Math.

Many of the C3 and NCSS themes draw on SEL domains including integrating personal and social identities; identifying personal, cultural, and linguistic assets; developing interests and a sense of purpose; and examining prejudices and biases. These topics prompt students to examine different perspectives and emotions, including examples of perseverance, optimism, and determination, and to illustrate social skills, including social awareness, good communication, and conflict management.

Illustrated texts in social studies include biographies of historical figures, accounts of historical events, and historical fiction pieces that draw on storylines of people's lives and experiences. These texts pull in aspects of all the CASEL competencies: social awareness skills, such as identifying diverse social norms, recognizing situational demands, and understanding the influences of organizations and systems on behavior; self-awareness; and self-management. Illustrated texts for upper elementary students focus on a variety of themes around identity in the context of social studies topics, including narratives around immigration, leaving a homeland, and adjusting to life in a new home; biographies of individuals or groups whose identities have been shaped by their experiences and who themselves have shaped history; and events—natural, man-made, catastrophic, and creative—that formed the identity of groups and individuals.

This chapter will discuss the ways in which the key aspects of social studies content can be integrated with SEL competencies and domains. Both the standards and the content topics within social studies are wide-reaching, touching on themes as diverse as geography, time and change, individual development and identity, science and technology, production and consumption, and civics. The chapter will begin with a summary of the two core sets of standards for social studies, grouping them into five overarching themes, and then examine how each theme can be integrated with SEL domains, giving examples of specific texts. The chapter will conclude with a book list and lesson plan.

Social Studies Standards

The College, Career, and Civic Life (C3) Framework has four topic-focused subsections: civics, economics, geography, and history. The framework seeks to make students aware of the past and the changing cultural and physical environments and uses an inquiry-based approach that includes four dimensions: developing questions and planning inquiries, applying disciplinary concepts and tools, evaluating sources and using evidence, and communicating conclusions and taking informed action. The C3 standards are designed to have direct connections to the Common Core State standards for ELA, providing rich opportunities for cross-curricular lessons and activities.

The NCSS standards framework is grouped into ten organizing strands:

- Culture and cultural diversity
- Time, continuity, and change
- People, places, and environments
- Individual development and identity
- Individuals, groups, and institutions
- Power, authority, and governance
- Production, distribution and consumption
- Science, technology, and society
- Global connections
- Civic ideals and practices.

The C3 Framework and NCSS standards offer a multitude of entry points to SEL themes. Table 6.1 shows examples of correlating the frameworks and themes with SEL domains. For example, within the C3 subsection of civics and the NCSS theme of culture, there are rich opportunities to discuss SEL competencies around identity—examining and defining one's own identity within familial, cultural, local, and global settings, and considering similarities and differences with other communities, across locations and time periods. These topics prompt students to examine different perspectives and emotions, including examples of perseverance, optimism, and determination, and to illustrate social skills, including social awareness, good communication, and conflict management.

By integrating the themes and standards of the C3 Framework and the NCSS standards, topics covered within social studies in grades 3–5 can be divided in to four broad categories: 1) identity, culture, and community; 2) history: continuity and

Table 6.1 Sample Social Studies Standards and Related SEL Competencies

Social Studies Standard	Sample Pathways to be Reached by the End of Grade 5	SEL Competencies
C3 Framework: Civics	• D2.Civ.2.3–5. Explain how a democracy relies on people's responsible participation, and draw implications for how individuals should participate. • D2.Civ.6.3–5. Describe ways in which people benefit from and are challenged by working together, including through government, workplaces, voluntary organizations, and families. • D2.Civ.10.3–5. Identify the beliefs, experiences, perspectives, and values that underlie their own and others' points of view about civic issues.	**Self-awareness:** • Examining prejudices and biases • Developing interests and a sense of purpose • Linking feelings, values, and thoughts **Social awareness:** • Taking others' perspectives • Identifying diverse social norms, including unjust ones • Understanding the influences of organizations and systems on behavior • Recognizing situational demands and opportunities
C3 Framework: Economics	• D2.Eco.1.3–5. Compare the benefits and costs of individual choices. • D2.Eco.2.3–5. Identify positive and negative incentives that influence the decisions people make. • D2.Eco.4.3–5. Explain why individuals and businesses specialize and trade.	**Responsible decision-making:** • Anticipating and evaluating the consequences of one's actions • Reflecting on one's role to promote personal, family, and community well-being • Evaluating personal, interpersonal, community, and institutional impacts

Social Studies Standard	Sample Pathways to be Reached by the End of Grade 5	SEL Competencies
C3 Framework: Geography	• D2.Geo.4.3–5. Explain how culture influences the way people modify and adapt to their environments. • D2.Geo.5.3–5. Explain how the cultural and environmental characteristics of places change over time. • D2.Geo.7.3–5. Explain how cultural and environmental characteristics affect the distribution and movement of people, goods, and ideas.	**Relationship skills:** • Demonstrating cultural competency **Social awareness:** • Taking others' perspectives • Identifying diverse social norms, including unjust ones • Understanding the influences of organizations and systems on behavior • Recognizing situational demands and opportunities
C3 Framework: History	• D2.His.2.3–5. Compare life in specific historical time periods to life today. • D2.His.2.3–5. Generate questions about individuals and groups who have shaped a significant historical changes and continuities.	**Social awareness:** • Understand the perspectives of others, including those from diverse backgrounds, cultures, and contexts. • Taking others' perspectives
NCSS Theme: Culture	• How does culture unify a group of people? • How do different cultural perspectives lead groups to interpret the same event differently?	**Social awareness:** Understand historical and social norms for behavior **Responsible decision-making:** Evaluating personal, interpersonal, community, and institutional impacts
NCSS Theme: Time, Continuity, and Change	• What questions are important to ask about the past? • What connections are there between the past and present? • What events and turning points are important in history and why?	**Self-awareness:** Understanding one's own emotions, thoughts, and values and how they influence behavior across contexts **Responsible decision-making:** Learning how to make a reasoned judgment after analyzing information, data, and facts

Sources: NCSS (2013 and 2010).

change; 3) geography: settlements and movements; and 4) civics, power, and government. These categories combine the two sets of content standards with a wide breadth of SEL domains and offer many opportunities for pulling in illustrated texts that bridge content and SEL themes.

Identity, culture, and community

The first topic in the subject of social studies focuses on identity, culture, and community. It includes the two NCSS strands of culture, individual development and identity, and global connections, and touches on many of the themes in the four topics of the C3 Framework, particularly in the areas of history and geography. Several of the C3 and NCSS standards focus on communities, looking at the roles and responsibilities of people and authorities within a community, how communities accomplish tasks, how people have tried to improve their communities over time, and the process of decision-making within communities and governments.

This topic helps students understand the range of perspectives by looking at similarities, differences, beliefs, values, cohesion, and diversity. It addresses such questions as:

- How does culture influence the way people modify and adapt to their environment?
- How have others influenced who I am and who I am becoming?
- How do the cultural and environmental characteristics of places change over time?
- How do choices I make influence who I am and how others see me?
- How are people, places, and environments connected around the globe?

One example of a text that addresses identity is the graphic novel *Borders*, written by Thomas King and illustrated by Natasha Donovan, which tells the story of a mother and her son who are members of the Blackfoot tribe in Canada. They travel to the United States to visit the boy's sister in Utah. At the US/Canadian border crossing, the US border guard asks the mother what her citizenship is, and she replies "Blackfoot," a citizenship that is not recognized by US or Canadian immigration officials. The mother and her son are denied entry to the United States. They turn back to go home, but after offering the same response to the Canadian border guard they are denied re-entry into Canada, leaving them stranded at the border, stateless.

Robert Smalls: Tales of the Talented Tenth, written and illustrated by Joel Christian Gill, is in a graphic novel series that focuses on Black American heroes in history. The title takes its name from an article by W. E. B. Du Bois in *The Negro Problem: A Series of Articles by Representative American Negroes of Today*. The three volumes in the Talented Tenth series focus on Bass Reeves, an escaped slave who becomes the first Black Deputy US Marshal; Bessie Stringfield, a pioneering feminist and motorcyclist who was the first Black woman to ride solo across the United States, during Jim Crow laws; and Robert Smalls, an escaped slave who became a Black politician and wrote and helped pass legislation that led to the public school system in the United States.

A good companion to the Talented Tenth series is the Toon Graphics graphic novel called *Black Heroes of the Wild West: Featuring Stagecoach Mary, Bass Reeves, and Bob Lemmons* by James Otis Smith, which is an illustrated history of the lives of three Black heroes in the Old West. A second book in the Toon Graphics series is *Paul Bunyan: The Invention of an American Legend* by Noah Van Sciver, which tells of the myth of Paul Bunyon, a lumberjack hero whose fame was propelled by a lumber company. Van Sciver's graphic novel contains a postscript by Deondre Smiles, a member of the Ojibwe tribe in Minnesota who gives another perspective on the legend of Paul Bunyan:

> When I was growing up as a young Ojibwe child in Minnesota, Paul Bunyan loomed very large in my life, as he does in the lives of many children in the state...It wasn't until I was much older and I was working toward my graduate degrees that I realized the story of Paul Bunyan,

> exciting as it was, hid the harmful things that colonization has done to Indigenous peoples and environments in the United States.
>
> (p. 40)

Civics, Power, and Government

The second category of topics covered in grades 3–5 includes two NCSS strands: power, authority, and governance, and civic ideals and practices, and standards from the C3 Civics discipline, including:

- Participation
- Rules/laws
- Civic virtues and democratic principles
- Working together
- Historical and contemporary means of changing society

Illustrated texts that support the standards include books such as *The Undefeated,* a poem by Kwame Alexander, illustrated by Kadir Nelson, which pairs Alexander's spare, beautiful words with images of the inspirational people and events of African American history, from civil rights leader John Lewis to artists Jack Johnson, Zora Neale Hurston, and Ella Fitzgerald; and athletes such as Wilma Rudolph, Michael Jordan, and Serena Williams. Alexander writes:

> This is for the unforgettable. The swift and sweet ones who hurdled history and opened a world of possible.
> The ones who survived America *by any means necessary.*
> And the ones who didn't.

These books address such SEL competencies and domains as self-management, which includes skills such as planning and organizational skills; showing the courage to take initiative, and demonstrating personal and collective agency. In the domain of social awareness, relevant SEL competencies include identifying diverse social norms, including unjust ones; recognizing situational demands and opportunities; and understanding the influences of organizations and systems on behavior. The competency of responsible decision-making aligns well with SEL competencies including identifying solutions for personal and social problems; anticipating and evaluating the consequences of one's actions; reflecting on one's role to promote personal, family, and community well-being; and evaluating personal, interpersonal, community, and institutional impacts.

Informational texts that lay out the facts and history of civics and government through colorful images and engaging text include *The Interactive Constitution: Explore the Constitution* by David Miles. For younger readers, David Catrow's *We The Kids: The Preamble to the Constitution of the United States* gives an explanation of the terms within the Constitution while also providing images (and a dog who acts as a guide through the text) that can help start conversations around the themes and topics. These books address SEL domains such as responsible decision-making and social awareness and open up discussions about how the laws and systems of government were designed and how we can think about applying and interpreting them through lenses of social-emotional learning.

History: Continuity and Change

The third category of topics covers curricular strands, SEL domains, and illustrated texts in the area of history, with a focus on continuity and change. Relevant standards from the C3 History dimension include:

- Compare life in historical times with today
- Compare developments that happened at the same time
- Explain connections among historical contexts and people's perspectives
- Describe how people's perspectives have shaped historical sources they created

In the NCSS standards, questions for exploration from the Time, Continuity, and Change standards include:

- What questions are important to ask about the past?
- What happened in the part, and how do we know?
- What connections are there between the past and present?

In the NCSS Individual Development and Identity standards, questions include:

- How do organizational and institutional affiliations influence personal identity?
- How do time and place influence individual development and identity?
- How do the choices that individuals make impact who they are now and who they can become?

Graphic novels and illustrated texts that support these topics range from biographical stories to historical fiction and broader histories. The French illustrator Barroux found a diary in a trash can in Paris that was written by an unknown soldier during the early months of World War I. Barroux added his own illustrations, done in somber, brown, black, and white colors, and turned it into a graphic novel, *Line of Fire: Diary of an Unknown Soldier*. In the book, the soldier documents his experiences and describes the mood and mood of his troop:

> From 05:00 hours, the battalion falls in. Our stay is already over. We move off in an eastwards direction. It's hot, the roads are hard and my feet hurt. Towards 08:00 hours, we reach Buissières, where an ambulance outside the town hall gives us a foretaste of battle . . . Once the rain has stopped, we head back into town to join our billets. The sergeant-major has found a small bedroom in a deserted house and, with some straw, it's fit for a king. No news from Paris yet. Time is starting to drag.
> (Barroux, 2014, pp. 26–27)

As a primary source document, the diary text is a compelling insight into the life of a soldier at the beginning of the war. With the addition of Barroux's images, the unknown author comes to life, and the experiences of the war are transformed into pictures that are much more vivid.

Another graphic novel that presents war through the eyes of the narrator is *White Bird* by R. J. Palacio, the author of *Wonder*, which, tells the story of the central character in *Wonder's* Julian's grandmother. She was a young Jewish girl who hid from the Nazis in a French village in World War II. The book aligns with curricular strands of history, explaining connections with the past and showing how the Holocaust shaped not just the life of Julian's grandmother, but generations of her family. It begins with Julian calling his grandmother to interview her for a school project, and the story then switches to the grandmother's voice and viewpoint. She hesitates at first, struggling to share the painful memories, then continues on:

> I should talk about it, mon cher. Even if it is hard. In fact, because it is hard. I will tell you the story, Julian . . . the whole story. Because your generation needs to know these things.
>
> Those were dark times, yes, but what has stayed with me the most is not the darkness, but the light. That is what I have held on to all these years . . . and that is the story I want to share with you now.

The next chapter begins with the image of the grandmother as a child, holding the hands of her parents, telling her story: "'Once upon a time' is how most fairy tales begin. That is how I will start my story, too, because my life truly began as a fairy tale." The beautiful illustrations show colorful images of her life, her village, and her parents before the war, then turn darker as the war begins, with images of newspaper headlines describing the fall of France, dark and sinister figures of soldiers in the streets, and images of the Nazi flag hanging on banners in the village. The images evoke the emotions that the grandmother relives through her narrative and provide a rich and powerful layer to the story that underscores the book's themes and offer myriad ways to begin discussions.

The History Comics series, published by First Second, offers historical accounts with colorful, comic-style graphics of historical events and important figures such as the Civil Rights leaders Rosa Parks and Claudette Colvin; the Stonewall Riots; the Great Chicago Fire; World War II, and the Transcontinental Railroad. Another graphic book which gives an illustrated presentation of the life and work of Rosa Parks is Insha Fitzpatrick's *Who Sparked the Montgomery Bus Boycott?: Rosa Parks*, which is a volume in the Who HQ Graphic Novels collection, published by Penguin Workshop. That series contains graphic novels on Cesar Chavez, Neil Armstrong, Amelia Earhart, the Dalai Lama, and Tituba, one of the first women accused in the Salem Witch Trials.

Broader historical perspectives written in a graphic format include such books as *A Day in the Life of a Caveman, a Queen, and Everything In Between,* written by Mike Barfield and Jess Bradley, which is an engaging and hilarious account of pieces of history from ancient through to modern times, with one- or two-page spreads often narrated by a character in history, for example:

> "Hi! I'm a sheet of thin foil known as a gold leaf. I'm in an artist's workshop somewhere in Constantinople in 537."
>
> "I'm Wu Zetian. It's about 700 and I'm China's first—and only—woman emperor."
>
> "Hello. It's summer 1941 in a town in rural France and I'm a letter 'V'."

Non-fiction and historical fiction stories about important leaders and events are excellent materials to support SEL domains such as self-awareness—demonstrating integrity and honesty; examining prejudices and biases; and having a growth mindset, self-management—showing the courage to take initiative, social awareness—identifying diverse social norms, including unjust ones; and responsible decision-making. Students can discuss questions about the initiatives that the leaders took, the ways that they showed leadership, standing up for the rights of others, resolving conflicts constructively, and communicating effectively.

Geography: Settlements and Movements

The fourth and final category of topics covers curricular strands, SEL domains, and illustrated texts in the area of geography, with a focus on settlements and movements. Relevant standards from the C3 Geography dimension include:

- How culture influences the way that people modify or adapt to the environment
- Population distribution
- Settlement, distribution, and movement of people, goods, and ideas
- Effects of catastrophic environmental and technological events on human settlements and migration

In the NCSS standards, questions for exploration in the People, Places, and Environments standards for the middle grades include:

- What "push/pull" factors influence the migration of peoples?
- How do changes in the use and distribution of resources affect people's lives?

Example texts that tie into the subject content as well as the SEL domains focus on experiences of immigration, including books for the more advanced upper elementary readers, such as *Illegal* by Eoin Colfer and Andrew Donkin, which tells the story of Libyan boys attempting to migrate to Europe and *When Stars Are Scattered* by Victoria Jamieson and Omar Mohamed, a graphic novel about Somali brothers growing up in a Kenyan refugee camp, as told by a former Somali refugee to the author/illustrator. In *Piece by Piece: The Story of Nisrin's Hijab* by Priya Huq, the main character, a 13-year-old Bangladeshi-American girl in Oregon, is the victim of a hate crime because of her headscarf.

In *Parachute Kids* by Betty C. Tang, three siblings and their parents come to the United States for vacation, at the end of which the parents announce that they are returning to Taiwan and leaving the children in California. The story is a semi-autobiographical account of the author's experience as a "parachute kid," a child who is sent to or left in another country without their parents. The dialogue is shown in white boxes when the characters are speaking in English, and yellow boxes when they are speaking in Chinese, which highlights the characters' bilingualism.

Biographical, semi-autographical, or historical fiction books about everyday people living through the hardships, discrimination, and occasional violence of immigration support SEL domains such as self-awareness: integrating personal and social identities; identifying personal, cultural, and linguistic assets; and experiencing self-efficacy; self-management: demonstrating personal and collective agency, and relationship skills, including resisting negative social pressure and developing positive relationships. Students can discuss questions about the decisions that the characters made, the bravery and determination they showed, and the way that they maintained their own identity in a new life and home.

The illustrated texts in the subject area of geography provide a rich foundation for teaching and discussing aspects of all of the SEL domains, starting with internally focused competencies in self-awareness and self-management, including: demonstrating honesty and integrity; identifying personal, cultural, and linguistic assets; demonstrating personal and collective agency; and setting personal and collective goals. In the interpersonal SEL domains of relationship skills and social awareness, these books address such aspects as demonstrating empathy and compassion, identifying diverse social norms, including unjust ones, and recognizing situational demands and opportunities.

The graphic novels and illustrated texts in the areas of social studies support elementary-level students as they begin to understand the political, geographical, and socioeconomic influences that have shaped their families' stories and their own racial, ethnic, gender, and cultural identities. The narratives and striking visual designs of the graphic novels and illustrated texts result in a powerful presentation that highlights varying narrative, assumptions, and understandings in the storylines or narratives. As a starting point or companion to subject content and SEL standards, these graphic works provide a strong foundation for students as they envision and create their own narratives.

LESSON PLAN

Title and Grade:
Borders: **How Cultural and Political Borders Define Our Identities** Grade: 4 or 5
Standards and Learning Objectives
C3 Framework: • Geography, D2.Geo.3.3–5. Use maps of different scales to describe the locations of cultural and environmental characteristics. • History, D2.His.4.3–5. Explain why individuals and groups during the same historical period differed in their perspectives. **NCSS:** • Culture: Theme questions for exploration, "What are important questions to ask about individual development and identity?" and "How do specific groups, such as family and friends, and attributes such as gender, ethnicity, and nationality, influence personal identity?" **Common Core Standards for ELA: Reading: Literature** • CCSS.ELA-Literacy.RL.4.3: Describe in depth a character, setting, or event in a story or drama, drawing on specific details in the text (e.g., a character's thoughts, words, or actions). • CCSS.ELA-Literacy.RL.4.7: Make connections between the text of a story or drama and a visual or oral presentation of the text, identifying where each version reflects specific descriptions and directions in the text. **SEL Standards: CASEL** • Self awareness: Identifying personal, cultural, and linguistic assets • Social awareness: Recognizing strengths in others; identifying diverse social norms, including unjust ones

Learning Objective
After reading *Borders* by Thomas King with the focus on the concept of identity, the students will write and illustrate narrative pieces that examine individual and community identity, discussing similarities and differences of identities, and describe how individual, group, and national identities may conflict.

ASSESSMENT

Informal assessment will include assessment of students' participation in whole- and small-group discussions and completion of the daily activities. Assessments will vary based on the level of the students; a suggested differentiated assessment would be:
- **Level 1:** Students will be able to discuss key details from the text, including characters and plot details. They will be able to describe the characters' identity as members of the Blackfoot tribe and citizens of Canada. They will be able to describe some features of a person's identity, including race, ethnicity, religious beliefs, and other features.
- **Level 2:** Students will be able to summarize the plot and use textual and graphic clues to describe the characters' emotions. They will be able to discuss how people define their identity. Can people have multiple aspects of their identity? How do individual and community identities differ? How are they similar?
- **Level 3:** Students will be able to summarize the plot and characters and discuss how national and cultural or ethnic identities can come into conflict, using specific examples from the book. They will be able to compare and contrast different types of identities and discuss the idea of conflict between identities. Why do the Canadian and US governments not acknowledge a Blackfoot citizenship?

LEARNING PLAN
Instructional Resources and Materials
Borders by Thomas King Interview with the author: https://www.youtube.com/watch?v=Aumxx1qn3uE Downloaded graphic novels in English/Blackfoot: https://usay.ca/blackfoot-graphic-novel Background materials about the Blackfoot tribe and people Lined paper and/or Post-it notes for note-taking
Daily Plans
Phase 1: Group Activity (1 Day) Begin with a full-group discussion of the concept of identity: • What is identity? • How do people define their identity? Ask students to define their identity by listing three attributes of themselves (categories of attributes could include gender, nationality, cultural/ethnic descriptor, member of club or athletic group). Then have them share with a partner or in small groups and discuss how each student's identity is the same or different. *Phase 2: Read-Aloud and Activities (2 Days)* Read *Borders* by Thomas King. The book has minimal text but it may take two or three class periods to get through it, leaving time to ask questions and discuss the illustrations. Ask students a variety of questions that allow them to develop their understanding of the key points in the text, including those that are directly stated and those that must be inferred. On the second day of this phase, small groups of students will re-read the book. If necessary, students can work with the teacher or teaching assistant. They can either be given a piece of paper to document their thinking, or they can discuss and share their discussion with the whole class. They will also read supplementary texts about the Blackfoot people.

Phase 3: Differentiated Learning (2–3 Days)
The goal of this phase of the lesson is to help students understand that each of us holds multiple identities, at the individual, familial, and community level. In some cases, those identities are different from, in conflict with, or not recognized by political institutions, as is the case with the Blackfoot tribe members in the book. Learners' individual needs will be met through differentiation of content, process, and product. Activities can be individually focused or complete in small groups.

Group Project
In small groups, students will study a component of the Blackfoot community or a leader in the community. They will create individual or small-group biographies with images and citations that look at the aspects of their subject's identity and how that was demonstrated in their life actions, decisions, and experiences. In the case of the Blackfoot tribe members, how did their dual identities as Blackfoot members within the United States or Canada affect and define their lives?

Phase 4: Revisit Group Activity (1 Day)
On the first day, students were introduced to concept of identity. On this final day, students can reflect on two aspects of the lesson: the physical components of a community and the human aspect of belonging to a community. Students can show others their projects and discuss similarities and differences.

References

King, T. (2022). *Borders* (N. Donovan, Illus.). Little, Brown.
Guns, M. G; Fingers, C. M.; & Guns, A. M. (2022). *Siksikaitsitapi: Stories of the Blackfoot People*. University of Toronto Press.
Smith, C. L. (2021). *Ancestor Approved: Intertribal Stories for Kids*. Heartdrum HarperCollins.
Speare, E. G. (2011). *The sign of the beaver*. Clarion Books.

References

Du Bois, W. E. B. (1903). The Talented Tenth. In Booker T. Washington (Ed.), *The Negro problem: A series of articles by representative American Negroes of today* (pp. 33–75). J. Pott.

National Council for the Social Studies (NCSS). (2010). *National curriculum standards for social studies: A framework for teaching, learning, and assessment.* NCSS.

National Council for the Social Studies (NCSS). (2013). *The College, Career, and Civic Life (C3) framework for social studies state standards: Guidance for enhancing the rigor of K-12 civics, economics, geography, and history.* NCSS.

Book List

Alexander, K. (2019). *The undefeated* (K. Nelson, Illus.). Versify.

Baptiste, T. (2023). *History Comics: Rosa Parks & Claudette Colvin: Civil rights heroes* (S. J. Grant, Illus.). First Second.

Barfield, M. & Bradley, J. (2022). *A day in the life of a caveman, a queen and everything in between: History as you've never seen it before.* Buster Books.

Barroux. (2014). *Line of fire: Diary of an unknown soldier* (S. Ardizzone, Trans.). Phoenix Yard Books.

Blas, T. (2022). *Who was the voice of the people?: Cesar Chavez* (M. Julia, Illus.). Penguin Workshop.

Bongiovanni, A. (2022). *History Comics: The Stonewall Riots: Making a stand for LGBTQ rights* (A. Andrews, Illus.). First Second.

Brown, D. (2013). *The great American Dust Bowl.* Clarion Books.

Catrow, D. (2005). *We the kids: The Preamble to the Constitution of the United States.* Puffin Books.

Colfer, E. & Donkin, A. (2018). *Illegal* (G. Rigano, Illus.). Sourcebooks Young Readers.

Fitzpatrick, I. (2022). *Who sparked the Montgomery bus boycott?: Rosa Parks* (A. Hayford, Illus.). Penguin Workshop.

Fitzpatrick, I. (2022). *Who was accused in the Salem Witch Trials?: Tituba* (R. MacColl, Illus.). Penguin Workshop.

Gill, J. C. (2016). *Bass Reeves: Tales of the Talented Tenth, no. 1.* Chicago Review Press – Fulcrum.

Gill, J. C. (2016). *Bessie Stringfield: Tales of the Talented Tenth, no. 2.* Chicago Review Press – Fulcrum.

Gill, J. C. (2016). *Robert Smalls: Tales of the Talented Tenth, no. 3.* Chicago Review Press – Fulcrum.

Gillman, M. (2022). *Who was a daring pioneer of the skies?: Amelia Earhart* (A. C. Esguerra, Illus.). Penguin Workshop.

Hannigan, K. (2020). *History Comics: The Great Chicago Fire: Rising from the ashes* (A. Graudins, Illus.). First Second.

Hannigan, K. (2023). *History Comics: World War II: Fight on the home front* (J. Rosen, Illus.). First Second.

Hirsch, A. (2022). *History Comics: The Transcontinental Railroad: Crossing the divide.* First Second.

Hughes, K. (2020). *Displacement.* First Second.

Huq, P. (2021). *Piece by piece: The story of Nisrin's hijab.* Abrams Fanfare.

Jamieson, V. & Mohamed, O. (2020). *When stars are scattered.* Dial Books for Young Readers.

King, T. (2022). *Borders* (N. Donovan, Illus.). Little, Brown.

Koch, F. (2022). *History Comics: The national parks: Preserving America's wild places.* First Second.

Miles, D. (2019). *The interactive constitution: Explore the constitution* (A. Pinilla, Illus.). Bushel & Peck Books.

Palacio, R. J. (2019). *White bird.* Knopf Books for Young Readers.

Schweizer, C. (2020). *History Comics: The Roanoke Colony: America's first mystery.* First Second.

Smith, J. O. (2020). *Black heroes of the Wild West* (K. Nelson, Illus.). TOON Books.

Takei, G., Eisinger, J., & Scott, S. (2019). *They called us enemy* (H. Becker, Illus.). Top Shelf Productions.

Tang, B. C. (2023). *Parachute kids.* Graphix.

van Sciver, N. & Myles, M. (2023). *Paul Bunyon: The invention of an American legend.* TOON Books.

Wang, J. (2019). *Stargazing.* First Second.

7

Integrating SEL and ELA

When thinking about how to integrate SEL and ELA using graphic novels and illustrated texts, teachers may find themselves with an abundance of riches. There are so many possible connections, and the narrative arcs that are a defining characteristic of most literary texts, as well as informational texts focused on people's lives, tend to show characters changing over time, providing a perfect opportunity for SEL connections. Additionally, in the upper elementary grades, students are often introduced to the different types of conflict (i.e., person vs. self, person vs. person, and person vs. society), and it is in managing these conflicts that the characters or individuals will demonstrate both their SEL struggles, and their growth.

When teachers and students ask questions about the books they are reading, they are also likely considering SEL competencies. For example, a discussion about a character's or individual's internal struggles, they are addressing the CASEL competency of self-regulation or self-management. Relationship skills are addressed when a class discussion focuses on how an individual or character manages conflict with others. A narrative about someone pushing back against societal norms or prejudices addresses social awareness. And, when upper elementary students begin to consider whether a person's actions were constructive or not, or where an individual could have made different choices, they are also discussing responsible decision-making. For teachers, the challenge might be how to narrow down the options, and how to find the areas that offer the most powerful integration which

DOI: 10.4324/9781003406662-8

engages learners and supports their learning. Information given in the previous chapters about choosing high-quality books, how to match children to books, and integrating SEL content in lesson plans provides a framework for these decisions.

State standards, such as the Common Core State Standards (CCSS), leave space for integrating SEL into ELA instruction, and also, at times, encourage it. For example, the introductory material to the CCSS notes the importance of creating an engagement with high-quality texts that "builds knowledge, enlarges experiences, and broadens worldviews" (NGACBP & CCSS, 2010, p. 3). The same books that provide powerful SEL experiences because they include complex characters or key individuals will often also introduce students to worlds outside their own, thus enlarging and broadening young readers' breadth of experiences through texts. Additionally, the CCSS specifically includes "social, emotional, and physical development" (p. 6) as an important component of instruction in ELA. So, not only is there room to include SEL in the teaching of ELA, the standards recommend it. Additionally, state standards generally do not require specific texts or pedagogical techniques, thus leaving teachers free to choose the books and teaching strategies that match their specific instructional goals.

Integration with ELA

The Common Core College and Career Readiness (CCR) anchor standards, which provide a broad overview of what students should learn in ELA from kindergarten through twelfth grade, serve as a good starting place for understanding how to make connections between ELA and SEL. These anchor standards are organized into four main categories: reading, writing, speaking and listening, and language, and each category has specific standards appropriate to each grade level which increase in complexity each year. The broad category of reading also includes the subcategories of literature, informational text, and foundational skills. This list of key skills provides innumerable opportunities for SEL and ELA integration. Just about any text chosen to teach an SEL competency could be aligned with an ELA standard, and conversely, for any ELA standard that is the focus of a particular set of lessons, a teacher could find a relevant graphic novel or illustrated text that addresses an SEL competency.

To illustrate this point, envision a fourth-grade classroom at the beginning of the school year. The teacher has decided to start the year by reading aloud the book *The Year We Learned to Fly* by Jacqueline Woodson. This book demonstrates how two siblings, with guidance from their grandmother, learn to shift their perspectives as they face challenges across four seasons. This book has a powerful message for students at the beginning of the school year, as students are both excited about starting school, but perhaps also reflecting on the difficulties they have had in the past. The SEL connections are clear, but there are also numerous opportunities to align lessons with ELA standards as the teacher informally assesses students' strengths and challenges in preparation for addressing them in the coming year. For example, by asking students to share with a partner an example of a time they had to overcome a dark mood, students will also be demonstrating the first CCSS anchor standard for speaking and listening, which asks that students "prepare for and participate effectively in a range of conversations and collaborations with diverse partners, building on others' ideas and expressing their own clearly and persuasively about particular text" (NGACBP & CCSS, 2010, p. 22). The teacher might also ask the students to write a short narrative based on a challenge they have faced or to summarize the story. Any of these activities would tie SEL and ELA learning together, and, on one of the first days of school, give the teacher a quick pre-assessment of the students' skills.

Approaching planning from a different perspective, teachers might begin with a particular SEL competency, a challenge the students are having in the classroom, or a contemporary issue and then search for a book that addresses that situation. For example, in recent times, the arrival of migrant families from different countries has made national and local news in many communities. A teacher might be looking for a text to help students who have been displaced make connections to others with similar stories, or for students who have not experienced such a traumatic event to begin to understand and empathize with those who have. *The Journey* by Francesa Sanna, is one example of a text that would meet this need. It tells the story of a widowed mother and her children who flee their war-torn country. The particular conflict is not named, but clues from the text indicate it was written with the experiences of Syrian refugees in mind. This book, which includes themes of conflict, courage, and compassion would address the SEL needs of the students, but also provide an opportunity for ELA connections, as students analyze characters and plot, support their thinking with evidence from the text, and talk and write about what they have read.

In this context, this chapter focuses on lessons using authentic texts that serve as a basis for the integration of SEL and ELA. We assume that teachers are also identifying their students' needs in such foundational areas as phonics, word study, fluency, and even handwriting. These chapters do not address these important ELA topics, but we trust that the readers are including them, as necessary, in their comprehensive literacy programs. As noted above, these can be supported and developed using texts that support SEL skills, but many teachers may find that it is necessary to give explicit instruction in these foundational concepts, just as they may use a specific SEL curriculum to support students' development. Our goal in this chapter, which focuses on the use of both literary and informational texts, is to wade through the innumerable possibilities for SEL-ELA integration and suggest some that are powerful and meaningful, within the context of a broader literacy program.

Table 7.1 provides some initial suggestions for making connections between CCSS anchor standards, specific grade-level standards for literary and informational texts, and the CASEL competencies. Obviously these are only a few of the possible areas of integration, and as you read, we imagine you will be thinking about the books that you use with your students, and considering options for integration with your specific ELA standards and the SEL competencies.

Text Exemplars

This section focuses on the narrative literary and informational texts that can serve as exemplars for integrating SEL with the

Table 7.1 Sample Common Core State Standards and Related SEL Competencies

CCSS Anchor Standard	Specific Grade Level Standards Literary Texts	Specific Grade Level Standards Informational Texts	CASEL Competency and Example
Reading-Standard 2 Determine central ideas or themes of a text and analyze their development; summarize the key supporting details and ideas.	• *Third grade*: Recount stories, including fables, folktales, and myths from diverse cultures; determine the central message, lesson, or moral and explain how it is conveyed through key details in the text. • *Fourth grade*: Determine a theme of a story, drama, or poem from details in the text; summarize the text. • *Fifth grade*: Determine a theme of a story, drama, or poem from details in the text, including how characters in a story or drama respond to challenges or how the speaker in a poem reflects upon a topic; summarize the text.	• *Third grade*: Determine the main idea of a text; recount the key details and explain how they support the main idea. • *Fourth grade*: Determine the main idea of a text and explain how it is supported by key details; summarize the text. • *Fifth grade*: Determine two or more main ideas of a text and explain how they are supported by key details; summarize the text.	Self-awareness

(Continued)

Table 7.1 (Continued)

CCSS Anchor Standard	Specific Grade Level Standards Literary Texts	Specific Grade Level Standards Informational Texts	CASEL Competency and Example
Reading-Standard 3 Analyze how and why individuals, events, and ideas develop and interact over the course of a text.	• *Third grade*: Describe characters in a story (e.g., their traits, motivations, or feelings) and explain how their actions contribute to the sequence of events. • *Fourth grade*: Describe in depth a character, setting, or event in a story or drama, drawing on specific details in the text (e.g., a character's thoughts, words, or actions). • *Fifth grade*: Compare and contrast two or more characters, settings, or events in a story or drama, drawing on specific details in the text (e.g., how characters interact).	• *Third grade*: Describe the relationship between a series of historical events, scientific ideas or concepts, or steps in technical procedures in a text, using language that pertains to time, sequence, and cause/effect. • *Fourth grade*: Explain events, procedures, ideas, or concepts in a historical, scientific, or technical text, including what happened and why, based on specific information in the text. • *Fifth grade*: Explain the relationships or interactions between two or more individuals, events, ideas, or concepts in a historical, scientific, or technical text based on specific information in the text.	Responsible decision-making
Reading-Standard 6 Assess how point of view or purpose shapes the content and style of a text.	• *Third grade*: Distinguish their own point of view from that of the narrator or those of the characters. • *Fourth grade*: Compare and contrast the point of view from which different stories are narrated, including the difference between first- and third-person narrations. • *Fifth grade*: Describe how a narrator's or speaker's point of view influences how events are described.	• *Third grade*: Distinguish their own point of view from that of the author of a text. • *Fourth grade*: Compare and contrast a firsthand and secondhand account of the same event or topic; describe the differences in focus and the information provided. • *Fifth grade*: Analyze multiple accounts of the same event or topic, noting important similarities and differences in the point of view they represent.	Social awareness

CCSS Anchor Standard	Specific Grade Level Standards	CASEL Competency

Writing-Standard 1 Write arguments to support claims in an analysis of substantive topics or texts, using valid reasoning and relevant and sufficient evidence.	• *Third grade*: Write opinion pieces on topics or texts, supporting a point of view with reasons.
	  a. Introduce the topic or text they are writing about, state an opinion, and create an organizational structure that lists reasons.
	  b. Provide reasons that support the opinion.
	  c. Use linking words and phrases (e.g., because, therefore, since, for example) to connect opinion and reasons.
	  d. Provide a concluding statement or section.
	• *Fourth grade*: Write opinion pieces on topics or texts, supporting a point of view with reasons and information.
	  a. Introduce a topic or text clearly, state an opinion, and create an organizational structure in which related ideas are grouped to support the writer's purpose.
	  b. Provide reasons that are supported by facts and details.
	  c. Link opinion and reasons using words and phrases (e.g., for instance, in order to, in addition).
	  d. Provide a concluding statement or section related to the opinion presented.
	• *Fifth grade*: Write opinion pieces on topics or texts, supporting a point of view with reasons and information.
	  a. Introduce a topic or text clearly, state an opinion, and create an organizational structure in which ideas are logically grouped to support the writer's purpose.
	  b. Provide logically ordered reasons that are supported by facts and details.
	  c. Link opinion and reasons using words, phrases, and clauses (e.g., consequently, specifically).
	  d. Provide a concluding statement or section related to the opinion presented.
		Relationship skills

(Continued)

Table 7.1 (Continued)

CCSS Anchor Standard	Specific Grade Level Standards	CASEL Competency

Writing-Standard 3 Write narratives to develop real or imagined experiences or events using effective technique, well-chosen details and well-structured event sequences.	• *Third grade*: Write narratives to develop real or imagined experiences or events using effective technique, descriptive details, and clear event sequences.
	  a. Establish a situation and introduce a narrator and/or characters; organize an event sequence that unfolds naturally.
	  b. Use dialogue and descriptions of actions, thoughts, and feelings to develop experiences and events or show the response of characters to situations.
	  c. Use temporal words and phrases to signal event order.
	  d. Provide a sense of closure.
	• *Fourth grade*: Write narratives to develop real or imagined experiences or events using effective technique, descriptive details, and clear event sequences.
	  a. Orient the reader by establishing a situation and introducing a narrator and/or characters; organize an event sequence that unfolds naturally.
	  b. Use dialogue and description to develop experiences and events or show the responses of characters to situations.
	  c. Use a variety of transitional words and phrases to manage the sequence of events.
	  d. Use concrete words and phrases and sensory details to convey experiences and events precisely.
	  e. Provide a conclusion that follows from the narrated experiences or events.
	• *Fifth grade*: Write narratives to develop real or imagined experiences or events using effective technique, descriptive details, and clear event sequences.
	  a. Orient the reader by establishing a situation and introducing a narrator and/or characters; organize an event sequence that unfolds naturally.
	  b. Use narrative techniques, such as dialogue, description, and pacing, to develop experiences and events or show the responses of characters to situations.
	  c. Use a variety of transitional words, phrases, and clauses to manage the sequence of events.
	  d. Use concrete words and phrases and sensory details to convey experiences and events precisely.
	  e. Provide a conclusion that follows from the narrated experiences or events.
		Self-management

ELA CCSS. Within the category of literary text in this chapter, we have focused on stories, although drama and poetry also fall within this category. We found that stories, with their clearly defined literary elements, including characters and plot, led to more options for integration, although there is clearly an opportunity to add texts outside stories to your book list for ELA-SEL integration. Similarly, in relation to informational texts, the focus is on biography and other texts that include key individuals and events. The texts described below were chosen because they serve the literacy and SEL needs of the diverse children in upper elementary classrooms.

Throughout elementary school, the CCSS emphasizes a balance of literary and informational texts, with the understanding that by sixth grade, and continuing through high school, students will need to be capable of reading increasingly challenging texts in the content areas, and be able to write in a variety of genres. As students progress through elementary school, teachers' decisions to include a variety of informational texts in the curriculum will help students develop the content, vocabulary, and text-structure knowledge that will be necessary as they progress into middle and high school, and, for many, post-secondary education. Wixson and Vilencia (2014) note that this reading "becomes the foundation, or the background knowledge (of the world and the words), students need to comprehend increasingly substantive, 'meaty' content texts as they move from grade to grade" (p. 432). Similarly, this background knowledge "of the world and the words" will also support students' writing development. The writing expectations will similarly increase as students move through school, and the knowledge gained from wide reading of informational texts will be invaluable in their writing.

Self-awareness

Chunky, a graphic novel by author and illustrator Yehudi Mercado, is the story of Hudi, a bi-racial Mexican-Jewish boy living in a working-class family in Texas. Because of prior health issues, his doctors are concerned about his weight, and his parents insist he participates in a sport. In his mind, he creates an imaginary mascot, Chunky, who is there to cheer him on as he struggles with body image, and conflicts with his parents, peers, and coaches who all seem to want him to be something he is not. Throughout the book, Chunky acts as his guide, encouraging him to pursue his ultimate goal, to be a comedian on a stage. When Hudi is having a particularly difficult time, Chunky suggests: "I think you would be happier if you went back to doing something that showed off your funny side" (p. 136). The self-awareness message in this book is a powerful one. To fit in and earn the approval of his peers and father, Hudi tries to change who is, before realizing that he is happier when he embraces his quirks and the things that make him truly happy.

Emmanuel's Dream: The True Story of Emmanuel Ofosu Yeboah, written by Laurie Ann Thomson and illustrated by Sean Qualls, is a picture book biography appropriate for upper elementary readers. It tells the story of Emmanuel, a boy born in Ghana with a leg deformity that made daily movement difficult. He learns to play soccer and bicycle, eventually cycling 400 miles across his country to raise awareness of and advocate for people with disabilities. Early in the book, the narrator explains: "As Emmanuel grew, Mama Comfort told him that he could have anything, but he would have to get it for himself." As an exemplar text for self-awareness, this book demonstrates how Emmanuel experiences the prejudices of others who think he will achieve anything in life because of his disability but does not let them limit him. He advocates for himself, and eventually for others.

The CASEL competency of self-awareness also provides a meaningful opportunity to connect with the CCR reading anchor standard 2: "Determine central ideas or themes of a text and analyze their development; summarize the key supporting details and ideas." For example, as students are identifying themes or main ideas, the details about characters' and individuals' traits and actions that are used to support their inferences can be compared and contrasted with students' personal strengths and weaknesses.

Self-management

Long Distance, a graphic novel by Whitney Gardner, is a coming-of-age story typical of many texts for upper elementary readers, but with a fun twist that makes it unique. Once students have identified it, they may want to reread the book, so they can search for clues in the words and graphics that they may have missed the first time through. Additionally, although race and sexual orientation are not explicitly considered in the text, Vega, the main character has dark skin, as do her two dads. In this story, Vega and her dads move to a new city, leaving Vega's best friend behind. To help her make new friends, Vega's dads sign her up for a summer camp. She is reluctant to attend until, while talking with one of her dads, she realizes he also does not have many friends in their new city. Vega then says: "I'll make you a deal. I'll go to camp and maybe even try to make a friend. If you do it too" (p. 36). In the end, after an amazing adventure, the story concludes with a positive message about the importance of friends, new and old. The self-management message in this text is about the importance of setting personal goals, such as making new friends even when it might be uncomfortable, and the value of personal and collective agency, both for the young people at the camp, and the people at home who were worried about them.

In *Going Places: Victor Hugo Green and His Glorious Book,* an informational picture book for older readers written by Tonya Bolden and illustrated by Eric Velasquez, the author tells the story of the creator of the *Green Book,* a travel guide for Black travelers during the 1940s–1960s that provided lists of hotels, restaurants, gas stations, etc., where Black travelers knew they would be safe and would be served. The overall narrative is one of an individual noticing a problem and taking action where he could. Victor Hugo Green was a mail carrier and used his connections from his job as one source of information for the book he published. The text states he was "vexed by the problems he and his people could face when going places. Inspired by earlier guides . . . he got busy problem-solving! From the grapevine he grabbed goo-gobs of information . . . He tapped his fellow blue-gray garbed [postal-worker] brothers for tips." One of the themes in this book is the powerful self-management components of taking the initiative and demonstrating agency. Victor Hugo Green went beyond noticing or complaining about a problem, instead creating something that made travel much safer for Black Americans, and also bringing customers to Black-owned businesses.

In reading these texts, and others that address students' self-management competency, one of the many possible curricular connections is to the CCR writing anchor standard 3: "Write narratives to develop real or imagined experiences or events using effective technique, well-chosen details and well-structured event sequences." The self-management competency focuses on how individuals regulate their thoughts, emotions, and behaviors as they react to an experience, which provides a meaningful starting place for children to write a narrative. In both texts described here, students have examples of characters or individuals making conscious choices to act in certain ways in response to a concern or a difficulty. In *Long Distance* Vega decides to try to make new friends, even creating a list of steps for herself, and at the end of the book makes choices that demonstrate she values both her new and her old friends. In *Going Places*, Victor Hugo Green uses the skills he has to address a serious need in his community. Using these texts as a starting point for reflection, students can write personal narratives that allow them to reflect on their behaviors and choices in challenging situations, or whether or not they managed their behaviors in ways that supported their goal attainment. Additionally, for teachers desiring a stronger connection to the graphic elements of the texts, students could create their own graphic novels or illustrated narratives, drawing upon some of the specific techniques used in the text of *Long Distance* such as font changes to show different types of communication or the scrapbooking techniques that are part of the illustrations in *Going Places*.

Social awareness

The graphic novel *White Bird* by R. J. Palacio tells the story of Julian, the boy who was expelled from school in the beloved novel *Wonder* for bullying Auggie, a boy with a facial deformity. The book begins with Julian video-calling his grandmother about a school project, while also expressing remorse for his behavior. The majority of the text focuses on his grandmother's story as a Jewish girl in Paris during World War II who was hidden away by the family of a boy in her class she had once bullied. In addition to the text, many of the novel's panels depict deep emotion in facial close-ups, and changes in the color scheme support the different moods and settings, from the present day to life before the war, to the trauma of being hidden away during the war. Social-awareness messages are clear throughout the book, including the importance of empathy and forgiveness, and the challenges of doing the right thing in an unjust world. The parallels between childhood bullying and the greater evils of Nazi Germany are also evident, with the grandmother noting: "It always takes courage to be kind. But in those days, when such kindness could cost you everything – your freedom, your life – Kindness becomes a miracle." This acknowledgment articulates the understanding that it can be difficult to stand up for what is right, even on the playground.

Separate is Never Equal: Sylvia Mendez & Her Family's Fight for Desegregation written and illustrated by Duncan Tonatiuh is an informational picture book appropriate for upper elementary readers. It tells the story of Sylvia Mendez and her family's fight for school integration for the Mexican-American children in her community. This text works well for use in a lesson that considers the social awareness CASEL competency because as the students are learning to empathize with the experiences of the Mendez family, and understand the common wish for children to have a quality education, they are also able to consider the specific steps that Sylvia's parents took with other members of the Mexican-American community to achieve the equality of opportunity in schooling that they desired. For example, Sylvia's mother says: "When you fight for justice, others will follow." This idea of collective action is an important component of the social awareness competency.

As students begin to develop their understanding of their own behavior in relation to others, which is at the heart of social awareness, they also begin to understand the concept of point of view. This is essential in addressing CCR reading anchor standard 6: "Assess how point of view or purpose shapes the content and style of a text." As students analyze the point of view in the texts above, or others, they can also articulate their perspectives and how these perspectives influence their view of what happened in the text. Additionally, students can also consider how the texts might be different if they were written by one of the other people in the text. For example, with *White Bird*, students who have read *Wonder* understand what Julian did from the perspective of the person he hurt. This consideration of alternative views can lead to fruitful discussions and writing activities in the classroom that support both the reading anchor standard and the SEL competency.

Relationship Skills

The Cardboard Kingdom is a unique graphic novel in that it was created, organized, and drawn by Chad Sell, but includes 10 others who tell the story of a group of diverse neighborhood children who transform themselves and their neighborhoods into fantasy characters and worlds with cardboard boxes. Chad Sell drew all of the artwork, and the bold colors and lines unite the chapters. This text serves as a powerful example of the CASEL competency of relationship skills, which focuses on establishing and maintaining healthy relationships and navigating diverse individuals and groups. While the overall message in the book is a positive one, demonstrating strong friendships among the neighborhood children, there are also instances of bullying and conflicts with parents. This provides readers with opportunities to reflect on both positive and negative examples of conflict resolution, communication, and teamwork.

A glance at the informational picture book *The Floating Field: How a Group of Thai Boys Built Their Own Soccer Field*, by Scott Riley and illustrated by Kim Lien and Nguyen Quang, might leave the reader with the assumption that it is a simple sports narrative. However, the themes of this true story, combined with vibrant pictures that capture the movement of the many soccer games, make the book an intriguing one to share with students. Initially, the boys who live in this remote island fishing village in Thailand could only play soccer on a sandbar when the moon was full and the tide was out. However, they notice that the homes in their village all float, so why not build a floating soccer field? The book begins with a quote from one of the boys inn on the team, who is now a man: "What's most impossible important is that anything is possible. And as a community or team, you can overcome incredibly impossible odds." Through their teamwork to gather their supplies and complete the project, the boys demonstrate strong relationship skills, even when they do not have the support of the adults in the village. These skills serve them well as they enter a soccer tournament on the mainland and need to use the teamwork skills and determination that served them well previously.

When integrating these texts with teaching the CASEL relationship skills competency, one possible ELA connection is the CCSS anchor standard 1: "Write arguments to support claims in an analysis of substantive topics or texts, using valid reasoning and relevant and sufficient evidence." In these texts, and in many graphic novels and illustrated texts that support the teaching of relationship skills, there are numerous examples of how people worked together or offered assistance, or perhaps did the opposite. In writing opinion pieces, the students can analyze the actions of the main characters or individuals, and write an argument, using examples from the text, about whether or not they believe the individuals demonstrated positive relationship skills. In *The Floating Field*, for example, the boys did not have the support of their community until the end, but they made choices that allowed them to move forward anyway. The actions of the boys and the community members could be a subject for opinion writing.

Responsible decision-making

Katie the Catsitter, the graphic novel by Colleen A. F. Venable and illustrated by Stephanie Yue, tells the story of Katie, a girl in New York City who does not want to be stuck at home while her best friend goes away to a sleepaway camp. Since money is tight, she decides to earn the money for the camp fees herself. She finds a job catsitting for a neighbor who has 217 cats all with unique abilities. At that point in the text, the realistic fiction story turns into a superhero narrative, and Katie finds herself wondering if she is working for the Moustress, the city's supervillain. As students develop their understanding of responsible decision-making, they can consider Katie's decisions, from her choice to do small jobs to earn money for camp rather than accept money from her best friend's mom to her actions as she decides whether the Moustress is a hero or a villain, and what she should do about it.

Becoming RBG: Ruth Bader Ginsburg's Journey to Justice, the graphic biography by Debbie Levy and illustrated by Whitney Gardner, tells the life story of Justice Ruth Bader Ginsburg, from her youth in New York City through her ascension to Supreme Court Justice. It includes her relationships with her family, her husband, and her children, as well as how the injustices she faced as a woman and a Jew, and the injustices faced by the people she worked with, influenced her and the causes that became the focus of her professional life. To address the CASEL competency of responsible decision-making, students can consider both childhood choices, like throwing pebbles off the roof of a New York City apartment with her cousin, or gathering foil for the scrap drive during World War II, as well as mature adult decisions. As an adult, Ginsburg had to proceed in a measured way as she decided how she would address the sex and religious discrimination she faced as an individual, as well as how she could best proceed as a lawyer and a judge in order to promote justice.

The CASEL competency of responsible decision-making aligns well with CCR reading anchor standard 3: "Analyze how and why individuals, events, and ideas develop and interact over the course of a text." As students describe or analyze characters and individuals in the context of specific events, their explanations can be expanded to include whether or not the choices made were constructive. For example, students could debate the advice given to Ruth by her mother, that she should be "independent" and that a "'lady' reacts calmly to upsetting things and without anger" (p. 26). While this advice may seem to be a product of the mid-20th century, students can reflect on how Ruth Bader Ginsburg incorporated this advice into her life and whether or not it is still of any value today for both boys and girls. While *Katie the Catsitter,* is a very different sort of narrative, there is ample opportunity with that text for students to discuss what a responsible decision is, particularly when there is not always a simple right or wrong choice.

The literary and informational texts described here all share one common characteristic; they were chosen because they move beyond simply telling an engaging story. Instead, alongside the story they tell, they share a message about how we want our students to participate in the world around them, including their classrooms, their homes, and their communities. With thoughtful integration, upper elementary teachers can use the teaching of ELA, which has a prominent place in every school day, to also support students' social and emotional growth. This chapter concludes with two lesson plans that provide examples for how to achieve these goals.

LESSON PLAN

Title and Grade
What can we learn from *Chunky*? Grade: 3 or 4
Standards and Learning Objectives
Common Core Standard for ELA: Literary Text • CCSS.ELA-LITERACY.RL.4.2: Determine a theme of a story, drama, or poem from details in the text; summarize the text. **SEL Standard: CASEL** • Self-awareness: The abilities to understand one's own emotions, thoughts, and values and how they influence behavior across contexts.

Learning Objectives
After reading *Chunky*, and participating in a variety of activities, the students will identify a theme in the story using evidence from the text, and make connections between their feelings about their gifts and challenges and the main character's experiences.

ASSESSMENT
Students will be informally assessed on their understanding of the story and the SEL competency through class discussion. Students can be formally assessed on the activities completed from the choice board.

LEARNING PLAN
Instructional Resources and Materials

Chunky by Yehudi Mercado
Clips from the movie *Inside/Out*
Sticky notes for annotations
Simple comic template (available online)
Lined paper and blank paper for choice board activities
Copies of the choice board

Daily Plans

Phase 1: Group Activity (1 Day)
Begin with two short clips from *Inside/Out* the 2015 Pixar movie, one from the beginning when the main character Riley struggles with the full scope of human emotions, and another from the end when she learns that there is a place for all emotions. Engage the students in a conversation about why it is important to recognize and understand our emotions. Students can be invited to share times they felt strong emotions and how they managed them.

Then the teacher will introduce the book *Chunky*. Using a class set of texts, or enough copies for students to pair read, students can read through the first chapter of *Chunky*, or follow along as the teacher reads. Without a close read, students may not follow that there are daydreams, and the introduction of an imaginary mascot, in addition to the more traditional aspects of graphic novels such as text bubbles, and shifts in location shown in pictures, but not text.

After reading through the first chapter for meaning, the students can then be asked to focus on Hudi's emotions. The focus question here is: How is Hudi feeling throughout the first chapter, and how does the illustrator show these feelings?

Phase 2: Reading and Activities (at least 2 Days)
This second phase will depend on how the teacher chooses to have the students progress with reading the text. *Chunky* is a fairly quick read, so over a day or two students can read the text, individually, with the teacher, or in small groups/literature circles. As students read, they can use sticky notes to keep track of their thinking, including questions, connections, observations about the writer's or illustrator's craft, etc. Periodically, the teacher can stop to ask students to share their thinking, or to ask "while reading" questions such as:
- What is the most important thing that has happened so far?
- What do you think will happen next?
- What are we learning from the text? What are we learning from the pictures?
- Do you identify with Hudi? Why or why not?
- What do you think about how Hudi is being treated by his peers, his coaches, his parents, etc.?
- What role does Chunky play in Hudi's life?

After the students have read the text, the teacher can assess the students' comprehension of basic plot points through a class conversation or a written assessment, such as a "somebody-wanted-but-so-then" summary frame. This will ensure that the students have the basic knowledge to proceed with the differentiated learning tasks.

Phase 3: Differentiated Learning (2–3 Days)
For this phase of the lesson, the students should work through the choice board activities. If the children are familiar with choice boards, and are able to work mostly independently, the teacher can use this time to pull small groups of students to provide assistance or challenge as necessary. A sample choice board is given below.

Third–fourth Grade Choice Board

Choose one activity from each category. Put an "x" in the box of the activity you completed.

Reading-Theme		
After reading *Chunky*, identify what message the author wanted the readers to learn from Hudi at the end of the book. Give at least one piece of evidence from the book that supports this message.	After reading *Chunky*, identify the main theme of the book, and then think of another book with a similar message. Write a paragraph comparing and contrasting the portrayal of the themes in the two books.	After reading *Chunky*, identify two different themes from the book. Provide at least two pieces of evidence for each theme you have identified.
Graphic Texts		
Choose two pages from *Chunky* that have contrasting styles. Pick two elements that are different (layout, color, font, etc.) and explain what you think the illustrator was trying to convey with the different styles.	Choose one page from the text to analyze. List three things that you learned from the pictures that were not stated in the text.	Choose one page from the text to analyze. Pick two different elements of the illustrations (layout, color, font, etc.) and explain what you think the illustrator was trying to convey with the choices made.
Social and Emotional Learning		
Use a simple cartoon page, or design one of your own, to create a cartoon that shows a time you accomplished something using one of your strengths.	Write a "somebody-wanted-but-so-then" statement describing a time when you felt a strong emotion and how you managed it. Draw a picture for each portion of the statement.	Write a short narrative story about a time you felt pressured to do something that did not feel right. Be sure to explain how you managed it.

Phase 4: Revisit Group Activity (1 Day)
This final day is an opportunity for students to share what they have learned during the differentiated learning time. In groups of three, the students can each share the themes they identified, their thinking about the illustrators' choices, and examples from the self-awareness writing/drawing activities.

References

Docter, P. (Director). (2015). *Inside Out* [Film]. Pixar Animation Studios.
Mercado, Y. (2021). *Chunky* (Y. Mercado, Illus.). Katherine Tegen Books.

LESSON PLAN

Title and Grade
Going Places: *How Victor Hugo Green and His Green Book Can Guide Us Forward* Grade: 4 or 5

Standards and Learning Objectives
Common Core Standard for ELA: Writing<ul><li>CCSS.ELA-Literacy.W.4.3: Write narratives to develop real or imagined experiences or events using effective technique, descriptive details, and clear event sequences.<ul><li>a. Orient the reader by establishing a situation and introducing a narrator and/or characters; organize an event sequence that unfolds naturally.</li><li>b. Use dialogue and description to develop experiences and events or show the responses of characters to situations.</li><li>c. Use a variety of transitional words and phrases to manage the sequence of events.</li><li>d. Use concrete words and phrases and sensory details to convey experiences and events precisely.</li></ul></li></ul>

e. Provide a conclusion that follows from the narrated experiences or events.

SEL Standard: CASEL
- Self-management: The abilities to manage one's emotions, thoughts, and behaviors effectively in different situations and to achieve goals and aspirations.

Learning Objective

After listening to *Going Places: Victor Hugo and His Glorious Book* read aloud, and participating in a variety of activities, the students will write and illustrate narrative pieces detailing a challenge they have faced or a problem they have sought a solution to, and the choices they made to address the challenge or problem.

ASSESSMENT

Students will be assessed informally on their participation in whole and small group discussions and completion of the daily activities.

Students' narrative pieces can be assessed formally using a rubric. Teachers may use a common rubric, such as the one used for the "6+1 Traits of Writing" or a teacher-created rubric that includes key criteria such as:
- Narrative focus
- Organization
- Elaboration of actions, thoughts, and feelings; dialogue
- Language and vocabulary
- Conventions

LEARNING PLAN

Instructional Resources and Materials

Going Places: Victor Hugo Green and His Glorious Book by Tonya Bolden
Opening The Road: Victor Hugo Green and His Green Book by Keila V. Dawson
Note cards with "What would you do?" questions
Chart paper/markers

Links to interviews with the authors and illustrators of *Going Places and Opening the Road*
Lined paper and/or Post-it notes for note-taking
Story frame or sentence starters to support the writing of narrative pieces
Assessment rubric for narrative writing

Daily Plans

Phase 1: Group Activity (1 Day)
Begin with a "think-pair-share" activity. First, ask students to write or draw about a time they were frustrated or upset about a problem, big or small, and what, if anything, they did about it. Perhaps they wanted a later bedtime and their parents said "no" or maybe they or their family members have been treated badly because of their race, sexual orientation, or religion. Then have them share with a partner, before asking several students to describe their experience to the class. Using the board or chart paper, create a t-chart that shows the problem and any attempts at a solution.

After completing the introductory discussion, ask small groups of students to consider "What would you do?" questions that align with the self-management competency.
- You've found out you are not getting a good grade in math, despite doing all of the homework. What would you do?
- You have a lot of homework, but it is the first nice spring day after a long, cold winter, and you want to play with your friends. What would you do?
- You want to try out for the travel soccer team, but your parents think it takes too much time and costs too much money. What would you do?

Ask each group to take notes on the discussion, so the new problems and suggestions for addressing the problems can be added to the t-chart when the groups have finished their discussions.

Phase 2: Read Aloud and Activities (2 Days)
Read aloud *Growing Places: Victor Hugo Green and His Glorious Book* to the class. Pause frequently to allow students to share, either with the whole group or with a partner, what they notice about the story as a whole, the author's word choice, and the illustrator's decisions to use both illustrations and primary source documents. Using Bloom's taxonomy, or another format to guide the development of discussion questions, create questions to use before, during, and after reading to develop the students' understanding. For example:

Before Reading:
- What do you know about Jim Crow laws or racial segregation in the United States? (remembering)
- Considering the title and the cover, what do you think this book might be about? What makes you say that? (analyzing)

During Reading:
- What are some of the challenges Victor Hugo Green faces? (remembering)
- What details have you noticed in the illustrations? (remembering)
- How did the *Green Book* help Black Americans? (understanding)
- How do the illustrations convey the time period for the story? (understanding)

After Reading:
- How did Victor Hugo Green's book impact the lives of Black Americans? (analyzing)
- How does the scrapbook format of the illustrations, including primary source material, contribute to the understanding of the book? (analyzing)
- How does Victor Hugo Green's story inspire you or make you think differently about history? (evaluating)
- Do you think the illustrations effectively complement the text and enhance the story? Why or why not? (evaluating)

Key ideas can be noted on chart paper so that students can reference them later.

On the second day of this phase, small groups of students reread *Growing Places: Victor Hugo Green and His Glorious Book*, this time focusing on the steps Victor Hugo Green took to achieve his goal of allowing Black Americans to travel safely. If necessary, students can work with the teacher or teaching assistant, or listen to an audio version of the story. They can either be given a piece of paper to document their thinking, or they can discuss and share their discussion with the whole class. Questions could include:
- What was the problem Victor was trying to address?
- What were some of the steps he took to address the problem?
- Who helped Victor achieve his goals?
- What challenges might he have faced?

After sharing their ideas, the teacher can conclude this phase by summarizing the general arc of the story. Victor Hugo Green identified a problem, and then using his vision and with help from his friends and colleagues, he created a book that helped make travel safer for many Black Americans.

Phase 3: Differentiated Learning (2–4 Days)
On Day 1 of this phase, ask the students to learn more about Victor Hugo Green and the portrayal of the story of the *Green Book* by reading texts and listening to media. The goal is to consider how the author and illustrator conveyed the story in the book read in class by comparing and contrasting *Going Places* with other portrayals of the same story before using what they have learned to create their own narratives.

Learners' individual needs will be met through differentiation of content, process, and product.

Content
Students are given choices of books and/or multimedia.
- Articles on the *Green Book* from Newsela adjusted to meet students' reading levels

- *Opening the Road: Victor Hugo Green and His Green Book* by Keila V. Dawson
- Interviews (either print or video) with the authors and illustrators of *Going Places* or *Opening the Road*

Process
Students will be asked to note examples of the writer's and the illustrator's craft, with an observation on one side of a t-chart, and their thinking about the reason for that choice on the other side.

Teachers can also differentiate the process by letting students choose whether to work individually or with a partner. The teacher or teaching assistant can also work with a small group to provide support or to guide students who could benefit from additional challenges.

On Days 2–4 of this phase (or longer if necessary), students will proceed through the steps of the writing process to complete a short, illustrated narrative detailing a challenge they have faced or a problem they have sought a solution to, and how they attempted to resolved the challenge.

Product
Students in need of assistance can be given a writing frame for narrative pieces that provides sentence starters and a clear structure. Students who would benefit from a challenge could be asked to create an author's/illustrator's note where they explain the reasons for their text and illustration choices. Students can also meet with a teacher or teaching assistant to provide additional support. Additional accommodations can include text-to-speech software, translation dictionaries, and the option of submitting a verbal response if necessary.

Phase 4: Revisit Group Activity (1 Day)
On the first day, students were asked to think about problems or challenges they have faced and respond to a variety of

"What would you do?" questions. On this final day, students can share their narratives. In addition to demonstrating the self-management steps they took, students can also discuss the choices they made in completing the visual component of their narrative.

References

Bolden, T. (2022). *Going places: Victor Hugo Green and his glorious book* (E Velazquez, Ilus.). Quill Tree Books.

Dawson, K. V. (2021). *Opening the road: Victor Hugo Green and his green book* (A. Harris, Illus.). Beaming Books.

References

National Governors Association Center for Best Practices & Council of Chief State School Officers (NGACBP & CCSS). (2010). *Common Core State Standards for English language arts and literacy in history/social studies, science, and technical subjects.* Authors. www.corestandards.org/wp-content/uploads/ELA_Standards.pdf

Wixson, K. K. & Valencia, S. W. (2014). CCSS-ELA suggestions and cautions for addressing text complexity. *Reading Teacher, 67*(6): 430–434.

Book List

Bolden, T. (2022). *Going places: Victor Hugo Green and his glorious book* (E Velazquez, Ilus.). Quill Tree Books.

Dawson, K. V. (2021). *Opening the road: Victor Hugo Green and his green book* (A. Harris, Illus.). Beaming Books.

Gardner, W. (2021). *Long distance* (W. Gardner, Illus.). Simon & Schuster Books Young Readers.

Levy, D. (2019). *Becoming RBG: Ruth Bader Ginsburg's journey to justice* (W. Gardner, Illus.). Simon & Schuster Books for Young Readers.

Mercado, Y. (2021). *Chunky* (Y. Mercado, Illus.). Katherine Tegen Books.

Palacio, R. J. (2012). *Wonder*. Alfred A. Knopf.

Palacio, R. J. (2019). *White bird* (R. J. Palacio, Illus.). Alfred A. Knopf.

Riley, S. (20XX). *The floating field: How a group of Thai boys built their own soccer field* (N. Quang & K. Lien, Illus.). Millbrook Press.

Sanna, F. (2016). *The journey*. Flying Eye Books.
Sell, C. (2018). *The cardboard kingdom* (C. Sell, Illus.). Alfred A. Knopf.
Thompson, L. A. (2015). *Emmanuel's dream: The true story of Emmanuel Ofosu Yeboah* (S. Qualls, Illus.). Schwartz & Wade Books.
Tonatiuh, D. (2014). *Separate is never equal: Sylvia Mendez & her family's fight for desegregation* (D. Tonatiuh, Illus.). Abrams Books for Young Readers.
Venable, C. A. F. (2021). *Katie the catsitter* (S. Yue, Illus.). Random House Children's Books.
Woodson, J. (2022). *The day we learned to fly* (R. López, Illus.). Nancy Paulsen Books.

8

Conclusion

The inclusion of SEL standards in K-12 curricula has steadily expanded throughout the last decade; all 50 US states now have SEL competencies included in their frameworks or standards at the pre-K level, 40 states provide support and advice for implementation of SEL curricula, and 27 states have SEL standards for all students in grades pre-K-12 (Kim, 2023; Mahoney, 2018; Stanford. & Meisner, 2023). But SEL has been drawn into the battleground of educational politics, with proponents and detractors hotly debating the appropriate place of SEL in the K-12 educational system. Even as more states incorporate SEL competencies in their curricula, lawmakers in multiple states are introducing bills to restrict or ban SEL materials in schools, arguing that the SEL programs teach students inappropriate topics such as critical race theory or sexual, racial, or gender identity topics and take time away from core academic subjects. Conservative activist Chris Rufo argued that the intention of SEL is to "soften children at an emotional level, reinterpret their normative behavior as an expression of repression, whiteness or internalized racism, and then rewire their behavior according to the dictates of left-wing ideology" (Gross, 2022).

In 2023, Oklahoma Senator Shane Jett introduced bill SB 1027 that prohibited the use of any federal, state, or private funds, to buy or use any learning resources containing SEL, which was broadly defined as

non-cognitive social factors including but not limited to self-awareness, self-management, social awareness, relationship skills, responsible decision making, and/or other attributes, dispositions, social skills, attitudes, behaviors, beliefs, feelings, emotions, mindsets, metacognitive learning skills, motivation, grit, self-regulation, tenacity, perseverance, resilience, and/or intrapersonal resources.
(Senate Bill 1027, 2023)

Several other states introduced similar legislation, including Maine ("An Act to Eliminate Critical Race Theory, Social and Emotional Learning and Diversity, Equity and Inclusion from School Curricula"), Montana, North Dakota, and Iowa (Abrams, 2023).

However, fundamental components of SEL, as defined in the Oklahoma bill and other legislation, are already deeply embedded throughout the K-12 curriculum without the explicit label of SEL. Good decision-making, strong communication, working effectively with peers, and creative problem-solving are fundamental components of curriculum and pedagogy from the first day of pre-kindergarten through high school graduation. Classrooms for the youngest learners have choice boards to help children learn how to consider options and make decisions; at the older grades, discussion groups and debate clubs help students learn how to listen and civilly respond to topics with different viewpoints; group projects require the development of good communication skills and a flexibility and willingness to adapt and compromise; and peer reviews give students practice in offering and receiving practical and appropriately phrased feedback to their peers. A classroom that is prohibited from teaching students about responsible decision-making, goal-setting, and organizational skills, appropriate social skills, attitudes, behaviors, or motivation, and self-regulation, perseverance, and resilience will not produce students who can function successfully in the world.

House Bill 688 submitted to the Montana state legislature proposed the banning of SEL in schools using the argument that SEL violated parents' rights to control their children's upbringing. In a hearing on the bill, teachers, administrators, counselors, mental health advocates, and parents spoke in opposition to the bill and in support of teaching and supporting SEL in schools. The range of voices and perspectives illustrates the many ways that SEL is used with children and youths, both inside the classroom and out.

Circling back to the C3 Framework from Chapter 4, we can draw on the call by the NCSS to pull back from political divisions and strive for a universal goal:

> Advocates of citizenship education cross the political spectrum, but they are bound by a common belief that our democratic republic will not sustain unless students are aware of their changing cultural and physical environments . . . There will always be differing perspectives on these objectives. The goal of knowledgeable, thinking, and active citizens, however, is universal.
> (NCSS, 2013)

With such a wide breadth of focus and purpose, books are a powerful tool to help students in upper elementary classrooms learn in a multitude of academic pathways, from practicing the skills of reading, listening, and comprehending to learning details of subject knowledge. Graphic novels and illustrated texts can provide information about core subjects, ranging from a historically important event or person, invention, or discovery to topic details explained in plots and through the dialogue and actions of the stories' protagonists. But the impact of these stories goes far beyond language and subject content learning, as these texts help students discover, explore, and define their identities and paths in the world.

The social and emotional skills that are demonstrated and taught through the text and images of illustrated books touch all areas of a student's life, from their emotions and interactions with others to their perspective, social- and self-awareness, and their sense of identity and responsibilities in the world. Through the actions of their characters, graphic novels and illustrated texts demonstrate cognitive skills, such as executive functioning skills, problem-solving, task initiation, and time management.

The use of illustrated texts offers a wealth of choices and opportunities in lesson planning by facilitating the integration of

SEL skills with content knowledge, offering opportunities to see and discuss SEL domains through the actions and dialogue of the characters, and presenting and discussing the topic details in ways that are culturally relevant and academically tailored to a wide variety of students. The breadth and depth of characters, life experiences, and plot points in the picture books of the last two decades has expanded enormously, offering innumerable lenses through which to view the world—whether that is a world that is familiar and comforting or new and intriguing for the students.

References

Abrams, Z. (2023). Teaching social-emotional learning is under attack. *Monitor on Psychology*, *54*(6): 6. https://www.apa.org/monitor/2023/09/social-emotional-learning-under-fire

Gross, T. (2022, April 28). How social-emotional learning became a target for Ron DeSantis and conservatives. *NPR*. https://www.npr.org/2022/04/28/1095042273/ron-desantis-florida-textbooks-social-emotional-learning

Kim, R. (2023, October 30). *A case for social and emotional learning*. Kappanonline.org. https://kappanonline.org/social-and-emotional-learning-kim

Mahoney, J. L. (2018, November 26). *An update on social and emotional learning outcome research*. Kappanonline.org. https://kappanonline.org/social-emotional-learning-outcome-research-mahoney-durlak-weissberg

National Council for the Social Studies (NCSS). (2013). *The college, career, and civic life (C3) framework for social studies state standards: Guidance for enhancing the rigor of K-12 civics, economics, geography, and history*. NCSS.

SenateBill 1027. 59th Legislature (2023). www.oklegislature.gov/BillInfo.aspx?Bill=SB1027&Session=2300

Stanford, L. & Meisner, C. (2023, July 27). Social-emotional learning persists despite political backlash. *Education Week*. https://www.edweek.org/leadership/social-emotional-learning-persists-despite-political-backlash/2023/07

For Product Safety Concerns and Information please contact our EU
representative GPSR@taylorandfrancis.com
Taylor & Francis Verlag GmbH, Kaufingerstraße 24, 80331 München, Germany